Believing
as
Ourselves

Believing as Ourselves

J. Lynn Jones

Foreword by Jeffrey Lang

amana publications

First Edition
(1423AH / 2002AC)

© Copyright 1423AH / 2002AC
amana publications
10710 Tucker Street
Beltsville, Maryland 20705-2223 USA
Tel: (301) 595-5777 / Fax: (301) 595-5888
E-mail: amana@igprinting.com
Website: www.amana-publications.com

Library of Congress Cataloging-in-Publication Data

Jones, J. Lynn.
 Believing as ourselves / J. Lynn Jones ; foreword by Jeffrey Lang.
   p. cm.
 ISBN 1-59008-007-6
 1. Muslim converts--United States. I. Title.
 BP170.5 .J66 2002
 297.5'74'092--dc21

2002003799

Printed in the United States of America by
International Graphics
10710 Tucker Street
Beltsville, Maryland 20705-2223 USA
Tel: (301) 595-5999 Fax: (301) 595-5888
E-mail: ig@igprinting.com
Website: igprinting.com

In the name of Allah, Most Gracious, Most Merciful

Table of Contents

Acknowledgments ix

Foreword xi

Introduction 1

Chapter 1: **Lap of the Muslim Community** 4

Chapter 2: **Dropping Out** 12

Chapter 3: **Going Home Again** 16

Chapter 4: **Beginning** 20

Chapter 5: **Prayer** 30

Chapter 6: **Sin and Despair** 38

Chapter 7: **Rethinking Sin** 50

Chapter 8: **Backbiting and Gossip** 56

Chapter 9: ***Hijab*** 72

Chapter 10: **The Ascetic Life** 90

Chapter 11: **Envy** 96

Chapter 12: **The American Harlot** 102

Chapter 13: **Arabic** 112

Chapter 14: **When Things Are Bad** 128
           A Note On Depression 135

Chapter 15: **Women's Work** 138

Epilogue 157

Acknowledgments

I would like to thank God for answering all of my prayers regarding this book, as well as those regarding all that I detail on the pages that follow. Words can in no way express, nor be sufficient in meaning to encompass the gratitude in my heart.

I thank my children, Ibrahim and Amani, for their sacrifice of countless fun-filled hours with their mother so that she may finish this book before they have children of their own, God willing. And thanks to my husband, who spent countless "bonus" hours with the little monsters...I mean angels.

Boundless thanks to the two people who went out of their way to support this book, Omer Bin Abdullah, Editor of *Islamic Horizons* Magazine, and Jeffrey Lang, author of "Struggling to Surrender" and "Even Angels Ask," who was kind enough to write the foreword for this book. They both expressed the true ideal of selfless brotherhood in Islam.

Special thanks to my sister, Jessica. Without her I would have given up on this book, as well as countless other battles.

I also owe great gratitude to my friend, Alice, whose thoughtful feedback made the difference between giving up and carrying on.

Finally, thanks to my family—Mom, Gary, Dad, Linda, Nana, Grandma, for always caring about me.

Foreword

The brutal attacks of September 11th have provoked intense American public interest in the religion of Islam. Like never before Muslims are finding themselves placed in the sometimes awkward role of spokespersons for the worldwide faith community to which they belong. Believers with a basic knowledge of Islam can easily field many of the questions being asked, but some of them reflect deep-rooted stereotypes that are not so easy to dislodge. At the top of the list of American concerns with Islam are the place of violence and the treatment of women within its system. Due in large part to the Administration's campaign to recognize Islam as a religion of peace, the first issue has been addressed as far as most Americans are concerned. Moreover, the vast majority of American Muslims appear to their fellow citizens to be gentle, good and well-mannered neighbors and friends, and certainly not prone to violence. Yet the image of Islam as a women demeaning religion endures and continues to be the main source of American aversion to the faith. Of course, the media has over the years played its part in fostering this image, not to mention textbooks, teachers and politicians, but I believe it is time that we Muslims move beyond denial and defense, and start critically examining our own behavior to determine if we may be doing something wrong.

A great deal has been written on the state of modern Muslim women, from sanguine expositions by Muslim apologists on their lofty status, to censorious depictions geared toward the non-Muslim world, to the seemingly dispassionate area studies of academia, to calls from many *ulema* for a return to traditional roles, to arguments from reformist Muslims for change. *Believing as Ourselves* by Lynn Jones, an American convert to Islam, fits in none of these categories, but instead broaches a subject of vital importance to the future of Muslims in the United States, and that relates to the very essence of religion: namely, it explores the avenues and impediments toward spiritual growth that Islam in America offers women.

Rather than discourse on Islamic Law or engage in the usual polemics, Jones reflects on the real day-to-day challenges of life after conversion that are unmentioned in most writings on Islam but that can affect one's spirit so profoundly. She chooses not to dwell on the opprobrium and estrangement from family, friends and society that many converts endure, for as unpleasant as these are, almost every American that makes the choice to become a Muslim expects them. However, very few who embrace Islam are prepared for the ills from which the Muslim community suffers; not that they are collectively worse than those that ail America, but rather they appear in unfamiliar cultural forms. Moreover, converts sometimes naively expect that since the subculture they have entered into is more overtly religious, its members should be less prone to human failings. They soon discover otherwise, for we Muslims, and all too often those of us that are most outwardly devout, can also be, among other things, gossipmongers, culturally chauvinistic, racially prejudiced, narrow-minded, intolerant, envious, materialistic, sanctimonious and downright mean. They also find that despite conversion, most of their own past weaknesses, and probably some new ones too, do not just go away, but still need to be fought. Add to this the growing disconnection that many converts feel from their own people, the many questionable and cumbersome foreign customs they are pressured to adopt in the name of religion, the normal trials of life and death and family that all of us are dealt, and we have before us a sure recipe for disillusionment and doubt. And while all of what is said here applies to both male and female converts, it is no secret that the women have it harder.

Becoming an American Muslim is not an easy transition for a man, but the road is steeper and longer for a woman. She has to make much greater changes in appearance, has to adapt to the female seclusion practiced at most Mosques and imposed at many community gatherings, and has to face a whole new set of culturally entrenched, woman demeaning views. The typical "ladies group" to which most female converts are shuttled usually offers little support or empathy, unequal access to rituals and community institutions, inferior facilities, and indirect involvement in community decision making through the married women's husbands. Yet the strange thing is, despite all this, the majority of practicing American converts are women, and from what I have observed, a greater percentage of male converts desert the community than female. Somehow, most of these lady converts summon the strength to persevere, or as the author puts it, "to hang on to their faith by the tips of their fingernails".

If I have given the reader the impression that *Believing as Ourselves* is a lament on the situation of female converts, then I apologize. Lynn Jones neither bewails their state nor pleas for reform. She does something more immediately valuable: she reaches out to them with practical hard earned wisdom and carefully thought out advice on how they can overcome the many distractions and hardships, and reclaim that "initial determination, internal strength, and sense of authentic faith" that once was theirs.

Most converts follow a certain characteristic path, beginning with initial fervor, followed by extreme conservatism, followed by confusion and despondency. For some the third phase is the first step towards further soul-searching, personal healing, and a deeper faith, but for others it signals their eventual departure from Islam. Many converts speak of feeling spiritually disengaged during this period, of being unable to experience the divine closeness that they had known earlier in their conversion, even though in all outward respects their behavior is in full keeping with community norms. Jones' fundamental thesis is that many reach this state because of a loss of self. She suggests that many converts, in their desire to win acceptance, try to recreate themselves according to community expectations, and to such an extent that they suppress their emotions, conscience and reason. When this happens a convert can seem strangely unlike her or himself to family and close friends, not just because of changes in behavior, which the faith may require, but also because of a change in person. Needless to say, such a transformation could be very unhealthy, but it also may explain the spiritual disconnectedness that converts report at this stage, because the means by which spirituality is experienced, the self (*nafs*, in Arabic)—their essential being—has been repressed. Jones seeks to help female converts that have experienced this loss by alerting them to its causes and its signs, and by proposing some steps and principles toward recovery.

This is a very important book. It is a beautifully written, compelling and honest depiction of life as a female American convert to Islam. The author shows great sincerity and introspection as she shares the tests and obstacles that she encountered in her struggle to attain authentic self-surrender to God. Although her personal experience provides the backdrop for her work, it brilliantly brings to light all of the common challenges to which converts are exposed, and provides poignant suggestions and counsel on how to effectively come to terms with them. Every convert, male or female, should read this book, as should anyone who cares about the future of Islam in America. I see it as much more than an expose' on the trials that face American Muslim women; I believe it very effectively illustrates the critical need to be first and foremost true to ourselves if we are to truly surrender ourselves to God; hence from this perspective I feel it would be of value to all who desire to grow closer to Him. One of the most important features of *Believing as Ourselves* is that it offers hope and inspiration to all those converts—and from the email I receive I know there are many—who currently feel bewildered and lost, and seek to rediscover within themselves the pure source of truth and spirituality that first drew them to Islam and that set afire within them such intense joy and love of God.

Jeffrey Lang
Lawrence, Kansas
February, 2002

Introduction

*The worst loneliness is
not to be comfortable with yourself.*
– Mark Twain

It's not easy to be a Muslim, dang it. Those who say it *is* are either telling a woeful lie, or have been conned themselves.

As for the rest of us, we have passed through the initial excitement of discovering Islam—and have realized that the heady euphoria of our early days has tempered to a kind of uneasy internal bemusement. The sledgehammer of reality has dealt out relentless blows of daily life among Muslims, and left us with a kind of fragility of faith, and an absence of the passionate internal certitude that we once expected to remain eternal. Our *belief* in God remains unshaken, yet our strength, authenticity, practice, love of Islam, and of life itself, suffers the effect of repeated abuse, self-sacrifice, and cold reality within the often thorny embrace of the "Muslim community."

We have passed through the stage of the fabulously incredulous stammer, "But...But...This isn't how it's supposed to be!" and have found ourselves standing in mute amazement at the ability of other, "newer," Muslims to be shocked.

Fights in the Mosque, religious one-upmanship, backbiting, spousal abuse, and cultural prejudice, not to mention the travails that greet us as "Western" Muslims alone, are no longer new, nor do they hold the novelty that was once so painfully exciting. Now, instead of furious incredulity, we grow quiet, sullen and resigned—and find ourselves precariously hanging onto our once secure faith by the tips of our fingernails, like a cat clinging to the branch of a tree.

As converts (or the more politically correct, yet patently annoying term, revert), we represent the triumph of the message of God in its purest form. We are the first of countless generations to embrace Islam, and, like the earliest believers in Mecca, face prejudice, persecution, and pressures innumerable from our own societies, friends, and families. Unlike those kindred predecessors, however, we often find the waiting embrace of the Islamic community less than welcoming. Instead of a haven of nurturing encouragement, where our faith should continue to grow and flourish, the reality of life among Muslims can be harsh, and the inevitable disappointment that results from that realization is bewildering as well as damaging.

We find that, while our knowledge of practice and proper appearance may flourish, the initial determination, internal strength, and sense of authentic faith seems to wither. In this reality, it is easy to become despondent, beaten down past the point of despair—for we wonder what it is we have lost—and how we have changed. We look back in amazement at our initial strength of faith and our ability to simply, and with integrity, *be ourselves.*

Amazingly, wonderfully, it *is* possible to begin a return to that part of ourselves that once housed the pure exuberance of those early days—perhaps not with the innocent wonder that once reigned, but with the wisdom, knowledge and experience that we have so thoroughly earned through time—wisdom that acknowledges the indispensable importance of authenticity to the maintenance of faith, and wisdom that recognizes that true spiritual growth can only be accomplished when we are honestly true to ourselves and who we are.

Giancomo Leopardi said, "People are ridiculous only when they try or seem to be that which they are not." I believe people are only capable of true happiness and integrity when they remember to be that which they are. In order to experience Islam as we once did, as pure, and as strong, we must bring ourselves back into the frame. We must step back in honest appraisal of the pitfalls and trapdoors of "Islamic life," be willing to turn within rather than without, and we must, as Matthew Arnold wrote, "Resolve to be thyself; and know, he who finds himself, loses his misery."

Do men think that they will be left alone on saying, "We believe", and that they will not be tested?
– Qur'an (29: 2)

Who ever is adequate? We all create situations, which others can't live up to, then break our hearts at them because they don't.
– Elizabeth Bowen

Chapter One

The Lap of the Muslim Community

For many of us, our first contact with the Muslim community is at the mosque. Who doesn't remember their first visit inside its hallowed walls, clueless, sweaty palmed and bumbling, we make it through that first foray in to the "ummah" and are still around to tell about it. It is no small accomplishment.

Ah, yes, I remember my first experience in the mosque with fondness.

I had finally worked up the courage, at fifteen years old, to venture into the small Islamic center in Corvallis, Oregon. There, I stepped across the threshold of the main door, and into the cool dim of the interior (quite probably with the left foot at that, *shockingly* enough). As my eyes adjusted to the gloom, I saw, out of the corner of my eye, a figure moving in my direction. I turned, and was met by a little man, rushing toward me with a wide-eyed look of horror.

Flapping his hands in a way similar to the manner in which one would shoo a stray cat, he exclaimed, "No! No!" "This is for Men! You go!"

Met with this warm reception, I beat a red-faced and hasty retreat, and stumbled to the back door of the women's entrance. I made my way inside, removed my shoes (you would have been impressed), and was promptly taken under the wing of a kind, American-Muslim woman named Amira, without whom I might have sat there unaided, only to rise and leave, never to return.

I told Amira that I had read the Qur'an, the classic A.Yusif Ali translation, for an English project at school, and that I believed in it and in its message of one God.

She said, "Oh, then you're a Muslim."

The Lap of the Muslim Community

A bit surprised, I smiled and replied, "Yes, I guess I am!"

Little was I to know how refreshingly uncomplicated and unpretentious this attitude was, and how lucky I was to run into this woman first. Many others aren't so fortunate.

I have seen the poor souls who, unlike me, have been subject to a veritable interrogation before being "allowed" to accept Islam. Then, upon satisfactory performance of said examination, have even been issued a "certificate" proclaiming their new and official status, suitable for framing.

One incident, at a mosque in Washington State, is particularly vivid in my memory. Then, a beautiful young woman, attending our regular Friday night meeting, said she wanted to become a Muslim.

That night, there were no fewer than thirty Muslim women present (more than enough to "officially" witness her *shahada*). Nevertheless, a flurry of activity ensued to locate a suitable "brother" to officiate over the process.

Unfortunately, the young man found it necessary to interrogate the young woman so mercilessly that, after finally "allowing" her to take her shahada, she was never seen at the mosque again.

Even after one successfully navigates the initial awkward entry into the world of the mosque, opportunities for embarrassing blunders, faux pas, and full-fledged conflicts abound. On the lighter side, we have to worry about such issues as whether fingernail polish is forbidden, if our scarves will flip off our heads in the middle of *sajdah* (an occurrence in which it is hard to maintain dignified composure be one victim or witness), and if we have enough Arabic expressions mastered to conduct ourselves gracefully through the experience.

In prayer and conduct there are countless intricacies that must be mastered in order to appear at home in the mosque. One must know that it is necessary to perform two *rakat* upon entering, with said entrance made only with the right foot, be capable of performing the *fard*, or required prayer in congregation, shoulder to shoulder with women who inevitably drift away, or conversely, packed tightly, feet to feet, with women who don't hesitate to offer a sound berating should one's pinky toe fail to achieve maximum pinky to pinky contact at all times. Then, one must perform the *Sunna* prayers (knowing how many to perform at that time), only after moving to a different position in the room.

All of this does not even include the marathon *Taraweeah* prayers that, during Ramadan, can test the balance of the most coordinated woman as she sways in lock-kneed attention, nor the much awaited, but often disappointing *Eid* prayer. There, sparkling in garish shades of holiday finery, women create a din so overpowering that any semblance of attention directed toward the sermon is a pointless endeavor, doomed to frustration.

Converts, myself included, often have an idealized perception of the kind of behavior to expect from fellow Muslims. Nowhere is this more true than inside the mosque, where, aglow with expectation, we bound forward, full of fresh idealism, only to be met with such shocking examples of rudeness and intolerance as to render all but the strongest mute, or reduced to tears.

I have been snapped at for such infractions as being unable to decipher Roman numerals with acceptable speed, "Its CX, how hard is it?!", met by blank stares and "Do I know you?", after saying "*salaam wa alaikum,*" and had my status as a Muslim put into question because I had the audacity to keep my English name.

My friend, Hanna, a kind and thoughtful woman, converted to Islam after growing up in an Arab-Christian family, one of the most difficult and courageous things to do on this earth. She braved her mother's tears, her father's vow of disownment, and the threat of physical injury from her uncle, all to accept the message of the one God that so many women from traditional Muslim backgrounds are lucky enough to be born with. Unfortunately, upon making her first hopeful entry into our small mosque, the one place in this world where she should have enjoyed a taste of hard-won belonging and acceptance, she sat in a room with approximately twenty "Muslim" women who curtly returned Hanna's greeting and returned to their conversation, as if she were simply a minor annoyance.

Hanna related, "No kidding, I sat there in the room with them for at least an hour, waiting for someone to talk to me or at least acknowledge I was there. It never happened. I finally stood up and walked out. No one noticed. I got my shoes, got in my car and cried all the way home. I have never been back there."

My most frustrating experience occurred after weeks of asking my friend, Nadia, to accompany me to the mosque. Smiling, we joked with each other on a lovely, sunny day. The mood was high, and I was thinking how nice it was to be going together to pray, and how she would see how pleasant it was.

Just as we were opened the door to go in, a voice from across the parking lot screamed, "Sister! Cover your head!"

Surprised, we turned to see a stern man walking past us, secure in having accomplished his duty of setting my friend aright, and intent now on going inside to perform his prayers. I am sure he was quite satisfied with himself. Perhaps he wouldn't have been had he seen the smile fade from her face, the dark turn of our mood, and the fact that, after weeks of persuasion, she would never again accompany me to the mosque, the very place where properly and kindly discussed, she might have developed a desire to consider "covering her head" of her own accord and conviction.

Of course, wonderful things also happen. Enlightening *halaqas*, beautiful professions of faith that bring tears, and prayers that, with the resounding "ameen" of a full congregation, can lend a sense of community and closeness with God that can be found nowhere else.

However, it cannot be denied that, although there are exceptions, many, if not most mosques and Islamic centers are not, to put it kindly, conducive to the inclusion of women.

American, European and other "non-native" women not only run into cultural, social, and linguistic barriers when among other Muslim women, but also run head-on into other messages, sometimes subtle, and sometimes not so subtle, that seem to say, "yeah, women are allowed to go to the mosque, but it's not really important."

This message is clearly and regularly conveyed by the glaring differences in facilities and services offered in some Islamic centers to men and women. Although, there are exceptions, far too many of the mosques in this country (and I strongly suspect elsewhere as well), are shamefully lacking in this area.

Too often, architecture and maintenance are painfully skewed toward the needs of our male brothers in Islam. Not surprisingly, usually the only ones who say this is *not* the case are also those same Muslim brothers.

Women are routinely admitted into the mosque through plain and decrepit back entrances, while men stride into decorative and, sometimes even grand, facades. Often the men's areas are kept well maintained and cleaned regularly, while the women pray in areas suffering from crumbling disrepair and neglect. Further, common services such as meals on Friday, and during Ramadan, are provided for men, while no such service is offered to their female counterparts.

In our own community's two main mosques, it is rare to find the women's entrances even unlocked during prayer times, and it is common to find the women's area used as an overflow when the men's floor becomes too full. Women are routinely displaced to make room for the "real" worshippers. Even worse, often the women's floor is used as a makeshift dining area during Ramadan, because, according to one brother, "We don't want to get *our* floor dirty because we pray there."

The community, as a whole, funded our mosque, after an exhaustive fund-raiser in which many of the contributors and participants were women. The joy and excitement we felt when we heard it would finally be purchased was immense.

Galvanized by the acquisition and excited by the opportunity to contribute to the effort of bringing the rather run-down, but full of potential, building to life, my friend and I shared an offer of labor and money to help fix up the women's floor with new carpeting, curtains and paint. In response, we were told, "It's not necessary," and that the money could be used for "more important things."

Disappointed, we relented and set instead upon working on bookshelves and donating books to be part of a library that everyone could use.

After a couple of weeks, my friend and I returned to pray, only to find, as usual, the door to the women's area locked.

Knowing the men's floor would be unlocked, and that we would find the key there, we ventured in, and were astonished to find new carpeting, freshly painted walls, and curtains. It was beautiful.

Excited, we located the key, ran upstairs, and opened the door to find that the same crumbling, peeling walls, broken blinds, and smelly carpet remained, along with a partially empty bookshelf, as all of the choicest tomes had been promptly squirreled away to the men's floor, where they presumably belonged. We were frustrated, disappointed, and angry.

What message women are supposed to glean from locked doors and skewed allocations of community resources, is a topic best left to psychoanalysts (although passive-aggressive does come to mind). Yet, the strength necessary to continue to attend mosques where one is likely to be made to feel unwelcome and unimportant, like an embarrassing detail to be accommodated only in the most minimal way, is not to be underestimated.

Although the resiliency of women as a group is legendary, it is no small wonder that most non-native Muslim women eventually drift away from regular mosque attendance, when, after years of continually butting up against walls of exclusion, they finally say, "That's it! I'm not going anymore."

This trend is not only sad and unfair. It is dangerous.

Not only are an unknown number of new and potentially new Muslims (of which the majority are women) turned off of Islam because of the chilly or non-existent reception they receive at the mosque, but, in not providing a place of welcome and inclusion, these women are routinely denied of the only place in a non-Muslim society where they can get any support and sense of belonging. When you consider the fact that, in the majority of cases, convert women are the first souls out of literally thousands of ancestors to embrace Islam, this is injustice (and short-sightedness) in the extreme. The simple fact is, the mosque is often the only island of safety and belonging a woman can find. If she is unmarried and isolated, where else can she feel a sense of community and support in the difficult path she has chosen—and, if she is married and a mother, where else can she take her children to show them they are a part of something big and vibrant, that Islam and a devotion to God is not just something practiced in isolation, but among thousands of others just like them?

The issue of inclusion is no small thing. Yet, apart from the occasional exemplary community, where the importance of women is acknowledged, the fact that women in general, and American and other "convert" women in specific, are simply not welcomed is a reality that is all too common.

As a result of this atmosphere, I, as well as every other close friend, made the decision to no longer attend the mosque. After spending a good portion of our early years as ardent "mosque goers," years of giving it "one more chance," forming and organizing *halaqa* groups, attending *juma'* prayers, arranging meetings, celebrating *Eid* and the conversions of many sisters, we kept running up against walls. Incident after incident, conflict after conflict, we finally all came to the conclusion, "It's not supposed to be this hard." We asked ourselves, then each other, "Does my faith feel stronger or weaker after being at the mosque?"

When, for me, the answer became consistently the latter, I stopped going. It was time for me to "drop out." Not out of my faith, but out of the façade I felt had been erected around it. It was definitely time for some changes.

So I do call to witness the ruddy glow of sunset;
The Night and its homing;
And the moon in her fullness;
Ye shall surely travel from stage to stage.
– Qur'an (84: 16-19)

You are the one who must choose your place.
– James Lane Allen

Chapter Two

Dropping Out

I must admit, I was a bit despondent over what I perceived as both my own and my community's failure. After numerous attempts, however, to attend and form *halaqas* (one, I recall, even disintegrated into a shouting match between a "leader" and a group member), and countless forays into the male-dominated domain of the Friday prayer, I had to face reality.

During the final months of my attendance, I found my faith and hope sinking low as I slowly began to admit to myself that I was simply "going through the motions."

While, outside, I appeared to be the "ideal" Muslim woman, inside, I was mired in a sense of utter defeat. Worse, when I recalled my strength of faith just a few years before, I was filled with bitterness.

When I finally resolved, like so many other women before me, to drop out of the Islamic community at large, I experienced a certain amount of guilt. I felt, because I began to turn down invitations to *halaqas* and gatherings that I was antisocial, unfriendly, and, also somehow less religious.

Although, I didn't know consciously what I was doing, I knew that I had to do something different.

I began ordering all kinds of books and tapes on Islam, looking for something that would help me lift my flagging spirits. I searched for anything that would offer some hope or validate what I was going through.

Instead, what I found was book after book full of what I call the "shoulds"—how things *should* be—how a husband should treat his wife, how a Muslim community should be ideally, how Islam and the "Islamic way of life" is the perfect way.

Far from being enlightening, these titles only intensified my despondency. What I, and many others, had experienced was so far removed from the ideal presented in these books, that I thought, *This is pointless. If this ideal cannot be achieved, then where is the meaning in all of this? Is it just one big PR campaign, all fluff and no substance?*

The final straw came when, one day, I received a music tape that I had ordered weeks before from an Islamic catalogue. The tape had been described as a compilation of "beautiful and inspiring" Islamic songs preformed by an all female vocal group.

Feeling particularly down on that gray and drizzly day, I popped the tape in my car stereo as I drove to pick up my husband from work. *I could use something to lift my spirits, I thought.* As the tape began, my ears were feasted to lilting, "beautiful" strains of "they're gonna go to hell...where they will drink boiling puss..."

In tears, I ripped the tape out of the player, rolled down the window, and hurled it out in to the rainy night.

"That's it!" I screamed.

The beginning of my experience as a Muslim had been filled with boundless hope and joy. I had a feeling that I was so close to God, that I experienced a wonderful peace and happiness. Now, not only was I filled with sadness and frustration, but I felt about as far away from God as I possibly could. For all the focus and time I had spent inside the Islamic community, I had lost the real reason I was a Muslim in the first place.

I finally realized that, despite all of the talk about God and Islam I had participated in and listened to over the last few years, it had been *about* God—abstract, distant, and distinctly foreboding. My once very real, personal, and comforting, experience with God that had led me to Islam in the first place had been lost.

Islam had become complicated and dark, filled with the conflicts and focus of people, including myself, that had their own agendas to follow. With meetings, people, and book after book, we filled every nook and cranny of our souls with messages focused on the wrongs we commit and the sufferings that await. There was no room for a balancing mention, despite a cursory aside here and there, about the hope and love of God.

I decided I had to try to get back to that place I had been in the beginning—that place where I recall saying to myself clearly one day, "If I die right now I am not afraid." It had been fourteen years since then, and although I couldn't remember nor hope to recapture everything characteristic of that time, It was so superior to what I was now feeling, that I knew I must be doing something wrong.

When, at fourteen, I picked up my first copy of the Holy Qur'an for a school project, I realized, perhaps only twenty pages into it, that I was a Muslim, and maybe always had been.

I remember taking that Qur'an, the classic and massive, A. Yusuf Ali translation, (the one I still use) with me everywhere. I even recall sitting on a beach chair next to the pool on my family's vacation to Disneyland, reading chapter after chapter, and smelling the wonderful scent of the old and yellowed pages, feeling as close to God as I have ever since.

During that time, I knew absolutely no Muslims. In fact, aside from the occasional television program, or National Geographic issue, I had never, to my knowledge, even seen a Muslim in real life. The Islamic community was something that I didn't even know existed.

I filled my days with the fun of the young, the quiet and inward knowledge of God, and my nights sneaking out to the backyard with a beach towel for a prayer rug and a bath towel for a scarf. I struggled to perform my newly learned prayers with a thin "how to" book in my hands, as I turned my face up to the stars and the warm summer night's breeze. I could almost *feel* the gaze of God.

Now it felt like those nights were as far removed from me as the moon. Though I had been "officially" a Muslim for several years, I was at the lowest point my faith had ever been. Lately, I would perform my prayers, but always find myself forgetting which *raka'* I was on. I hadn't picked up my Qur'an for literally months, and I found myself dusting off the cover on my housekeeping rounds, lest someone notice how infrequently it was read.

Then one day, as I sat at the kitchen table, drinking my favorite coffee, and feeling the morning sun as it streamed through the windows, I thought, *Ok, you tried all of these activities. You did the mosque, the community, and the social "thing," and it didn't work. Maybe your focus was wrong. Maybe you can go back to it and have a fresh start later, but not now, not until you repair your outlook and your mind. Not until you excavate that strength of faith that made you a Muslim in the first place.*

Thus, I began.

*O thou man! Verily thou art ever
Toiling on towards thy Lord—
Painfully Toiling…*

– Qur'an (84: 6)

*No matter how far you have gone
on a wrong road, turn back.*

– Turkish Proverb

Chapter Three
Going Home Again

"Go back, go back, go back...Go back to where you were."

My son was watching his favorite program, Nickelodeon's *Blue's Clues*. Steve, the host, was singing the little tune, teaching what you should do when you lose something.

The song reminded me of one of my more frustrating habits, one that absolutely refuses to budge from my well-stocked bad-habit repertoire, despite my best (half-hearted) efforts.

Again and again, always when I am late and rushing, I discover that I don't have my car keys and am required to mentally retrace where I tossed them last.

This habit irks my, usually patient, husband to no end. He, with his characteristically "logical" male mind, cannot fathom why I would not learn from my mistake and habitually leave my keys in a designated location. (This is also the same husband who courts divorce each time he forgets to return the toilet seat to its proper position, and I, feet flailing, and fingers splayed in alarm, struggle to extricate myself from said commode.)

Is there any difference between loosing something, like a backpack or a pair of glasses, and trying to recall where it was you placed it, and something more internal, like love, friendship, or even faith? Can you simply "go back to where you were?"

They say you can never go home again, and I assume that means that a certain part of the experience of "being home" is lost forever in the act of growing up, in taking on the responsibilities and experiences of adult life.

Going Home Again

Any "returned child" can agree that going home to one's parents or family home for a visit, or even a prolonged stay, never holds quite the same charm as a childhood remembered. It can, however, bring back memories and shadows of those feelings that were experienced in the situations and places of childhood. It also seems that those visits home somehow, at their conclusion, lend a certain breath of fresh air and vigor to us when we return to our adult lives.

I believe that experience of "going home" is no different from going home to that place within, where faith was once at its highest, that place, for many of us when we "accepted Islam"—not the official, "*shahada* moment," but that first twinge of *internal* acknowledgement—when we knew *inside* that we were Muslim.

If you have made it this far, and have remained a Muslim through the ups and downs of "Islamic life," chances are your initial decision (if you can call it a decision), better, your internal *knowing* that Islam was true and real, was a deeply personal experience.

Although Muslim friends may have surrounded you, perhaps a husband, or dare I say it, a significant other, may have encouraged your consideration of Islam, the conviction was your own. Even, perhaps, like me, you didn't know any Muslims, and, instead, found Islam though reading. Either way, the conviction was yours and yours alone. It only makes sense that a re-awakening (or perhaps re-charging) of faith should, and, in fact, *must* be a solitary one.

When I say solitary, I don't mean completely cut off. The simple fact is, many, if not most of us, have a family and children to care for. I know I do. But, going back to the sweetest root of faith, when a noticeable departure has occurred over time, necessitates a certain willingness to stand back from the way we have been living our lives. It requires a shift in focus, first internally, then bit by bit in stolen moments, externally to ourselves.

You may protest, "Now, wait just a minute..." "Isn't that selfish?" "Isn't the whole point of this to be focusing again on God?"

The answer is yes to both questions.

It is selfish. But not in the way you think.

It is not a negative thing to focus on the self. It is a necessary thing, a beautiful and a good thing.

As women, we have been conditioned to be self-less, a word that, if you consider its meaning implies, "no self," and emptiness.

It is no accident that when many women examine their feelings about themselves, they often put "emptiness" at the top of the list of words that come to mind. This begs the question—How can an empty person, one with no sense of "self" have a meaningful relationship to God and faith? Under such conditions it is all but impossible.

It is very popular to talk about *jihad* of the *nafs*, the inner spiritual battle of every Muslim. Too often, however, lectures on this topic can be nauseatingly preachy and overdone, or, worse yet, only mentioned when *jihad* itself (in its more literal sense) is being discussed, as a way of assuaging guilt over not actively participating in the struggle in places like Chechnya, Bosnia, or Palestine. We hear, "*Jihad*...yes, it is important, but first we must focus on *jihad* of the *nafs*!" It is a familiar refrain, with little or no follow-up on just *how* such an endeavor might be accomplished. For these reasons, and for the very real linguistic component, I prefer not to call this experience of "turning inward" or the search for self a "*jihad* of the *nafs*."

Dr. Phil McGraw writes in his popular book, *Life Strategies*, "You've got to name it to claim it." If you are internally fluent in Arabic, and it really means something to you, by all means, use *jihad* of the *nafs*. If you think and dream in English, however (or any other language), I urge you to devise a term of your own to name your quest (*I like to call it an internal pilgrimage.*) If you think this hokey or otherwise find it does not resonate with you, find your own. But I do urge you to "name it" to lend a sense of authenticity and reality to the process.

Barbara Grizzuti Harrison said, "All acts performed in the world begin in the imagination." — Naming your greatest journey allows you to begin.

*... And He found thee wandering,
and He gave thee guidance.*
– Qur'an (93: 7)

*Pilgrims are persons in motion passing through territories
not their own-seeking something we might call completion,
or perhaps the word clarity will do as well,
a goal to which only the spirit's compass points the way.*

– Richard Niebuhr

Chapter Four

Beginning

There is a rich tradition of pilgrimage in Islam that has nothing to do with *Hajj*.

From Abraham to Moses, Jesus to Muhammad, prophets and regular souls, alike, have strived through solitary contemplation on mountains, in caves, in deserts, and, I suspect, kitchens innumerable, to develop faith of strength, true integrity, and authenticity.

Converts are, indeed, close to their illustrious predecessors in their individual quests for the true God. For they, through true and yearning contemplation have experienced the "lifting of the veil of truth" in a way never to be experienced by those blessed by a Muslim upbringing.

It is perhaps because of this experience, and the remembrance of the joy of discovering Islam—that first surge of faith, strong as a blast furnace that we often feel the most despair and loss when the inevitable tide of daily life erodes away some of its initial intensity.

We often feel lost, confused, discouraged, and even bitter when the tide of enthusiasm, previously untried by reality, ebbs. When personal factors combine with the very human (and fallible) Muslim experience, and we encounter the often difficult and challenging milestones of life, marriage, birth, death—daily joys and strife—true faith is tested, alternately strained and reinforced, in ways completely unexpected in our early days of faithful euphoria.

The sad thing is, we often feel a sense of failure when this stage inevitably comes, as it naturally does for us all. No one tells us that it is a normal process of growth, not a personal defect of character or faith. It is therefore helpful to know that there is a method, tried and true by the most illustrious of souls, to buoy the most flagging of spirits; a way to find a level of faith and contentment previously thought lost.

Beginning

Personal pilgrimage, a private search to regain faith and peace, is amazingly effective. Turning inward to the spirit can enable us to embark on an inner journey that is as meaningful, important, and ultimately as wonderful as any experience we will undertake.

In order to begin, it is absolutely essential to take some time for yourself. Yet it is often hard to do, especially for those of us who have families.

You may say, "But...I don't have any time to myself. The demands of my family, my children, don't allow for that. I simply don't have any free time."

That is probably true. I know it was, and still is for me.

I have two children, a three year old, and a ten month old, a husband (who came from a very small village where the mark of a "good" woman is her ability to serve until exhaustion), and an elderly mother-in law. Believe me, I never just "have" free time. Those days were gone long ago.

What I do have is the determination to *actively* take time for myself.

Alexandra Stoddard, in her beautiful book, *Mothers; a Celebration*, says, "No one ever gives us time. We never find time—we must seize time."

She is absolutely right.

If you are waiting for a husband, child, or any other person in your life that you love to say, "oh, yes, mommy, dear, (or fill in the blank), take time away from my needs and wants and go spend time on yourself," you will be waiting a very long time indeed! That's not to say that family members don't love and care for us. On the contrary, they probably care immensely.

The simple fact is, resistance to change is a normal, human fact of life. If your family is used to you giving every drop of yourself to them and their needs, they will notice, and will resist the change. Even though they don't need every atom of what you have to offer, they will want what they are used to, even if they or *you* don't consciously realize it.

The peerless rewards of taking time back for yourself, rewards of spiritual and emotional fulfillment, a sense of wholeness and vibrancy—create a person internally healthy enough to have a strong faith in God. It is well worth the effort, as well as the initial unease. In being happier, and more autonomous *within*, you actually become a better mother, wife, and friend, than you ever could have been when you were giving away every drop of yourself to others.

Mothers are often the most resistant to taking time for themselves, not because they dislike the idea, but are, instead, so mired in habits of guilt and selflessness, that they feel genuinely unable to escape from the endless demands of motherhood.

It often takes experience born of a full-blown burnout to recognize the indispensable importance of self-care to successful motherhood—as Carl Jung wrote, "Nothing has a stronger influence psychologically on their environment and especially on their children than the unlived life of the parent." A child with a happy and whole parent is a happier and ultimately more secure child. Still further, a mother who takes time for herself makes herself a better mother, and even, if she is married, a better wife—for, as the famous relationship therapist, Judith Sills writes, "…the better you feel about yourself, the fewer limits you will place on your ability to love."

I found that, before I began my own "inner pilgrimage," when I was living with an exclusive outward focus toward community, family, and friends, not only was my faith at a horribly low point, but my happiness and connection with my husband was as well. In fact, all of my relationships with friends were also extremely unsatisfying. I found myself saying things like, "I have so many 'friends,' but I don't feel truly close to any of them." Every friendship seemed superficial, and, well, fake.

I further began to recognize that the most common feeling I experienced in my friendships was resentment as well, a fact I often communicated to my husband, saying, "Oh…She just wants to be my friend because she wants something from me."

I remember going through a period with my husband when I felt I didn't have it in me to extend any extra effort for him. One point I recall vividly. He had an extremely bad cold and was lying on the couch. I made him tea, brought him a warm blanket and made him comfortable. What was alarming was the realization that, inside, instead of feeling sympathy and happiness that I was helping him to feel better, I was actually feeling resentment that yet one more demand was being made upon me.

Beginning

It took a long time to realize that it wasn't other people—my friends, or my husband that were fake or opportunistic in their relationships with me. Although it was true that many of my friendships consisted only of a seemingly never-ending series of favors, or sessions acting as an emotional "sounding board," the fact that I never felt a real sense of closeness or connection had a lot to do with me. The simple truth was, other than my ability give either with physical work, or emotional empathy, there was no "real me" to know.

Michael J. Gelb wrote, "In order to be in touch with someone else you must first be in touch with yourself." In neglecting to take the time, in failing to seize it, in order to spend time on the real me, I actually created the *impossibility* of possessing a true friendship, satisfying marriage, or the best possible relationship with my children. After all, as an empty shell of myself, what was I really bringing to the table?

How, then, do you go about taking time for yourself in the real world? If, like I was, you are not used to it, the idea can be quite daunting, and you might discover that finding large blocks of time seems to be close to impossible. As a matter of fact, the weekend, usually touted as the time officially sanctioned as "time off," is my busiest family time of the week. More practical opportunities for taking time for myself are in the early morning, or the late evening. In fact, I usually take both.

If, for some reason, you cannot take the time in the morning or evening, and you have no suitable replacement time, say, in the afternoon, you will have to take several mini-periods during the day whenever you can find them. After beginning the process, however, I think you will find that you really enjoy it so much, you will become better at seizing those larger blocks of time that you really need.

You may ask, "What do I do with all this free time?" "Pray?" "Read Qur'an?"

The answer is no. Do those things, but not during those blocks of time that are "yours." What I suggest, and what has worked for me is to do two things.

The first of these two "tasks" sounds very simple—and it is. It may even sound silly. Simply, you should spend time quietly and preferably alone (the only exception in my opinion should be a nursing baby that is too small to be left with someone else) *doing something you absolutely love*. It can't be something that you *should love*—that's why I exclude praying and reading Qur'an. Lets face it. If you loved doing those things your faith, by definition, would not be low.

The only rule here is that your time be spent on something that is absolutely one of your passions. If you love reading, go to a great bookstore, get a cup of coffee and just read. If you love writing, write, gardening, karate, crafts, *anything* as long as you truly love it. It is not necessary that you write it in stone. If you have a few favorite passions, switch at will.

A common problem is that many women have trouble thinking of what it is that they love. This is hardly surprising. It simply means that you have gone for so long in your self-less mode that you can't recall how it feels to return to a love. If you find yourself in this situation, ask yourself the following questions,

– When am I happiest?
– What do I enjoy?
– What have I always wanted to do?

Go to a bookstore, and notice what kinds of books you are drawn to...novels, mysteries, non-fiction? What kind of books do you seek within these categories? What does this say about your interests? If you are married, spend some quiet time recalling what it was you were interested in before you married.

The second necessary task is a physical one.

You must walk.

You may ask, "What do you mean walk? What does that have to do with regaining a sense of self and faith?"

Plenty, but I don't mean the kind of walking you think.

I am not referring to walking for aerobic exercise (although it is definitely a pleasant side benefit), or the kind with hand weights, grimaced expressions of exertion, special shoes or treadmills.

I mean walking as a way of recharging your spirit and waking up awareness. It may sound silly, and a bit "new-age," but, walking to gain inner peace and insight is as old as time. The philosopher, Saint Augustine, wrote, "*Salvitor ambulando*," which means, "It is solved by walking." Surprisingly enough, he is right.

There is something inexplicable about being out, ambling through the neighborhood, country, or even the city streets, that seems to bring a peace, clarity of emotion and sense of well-being that cannot be accomplished as easily in any other way. When we remain inside for extended periods of time, it is easy to lose perspective in our lives, and our problems. We lose connection with the bigger world around us. By "the bigger world," I do not mean *people* alone, but the world as a whole—nature, the people around, the place created by God were we belong that is bigger than our day-to-day "life of details."

"Earth with her thousand voices praises God"—Samuel Taylor Coleridge knew the benefits of "stepping out" into the world. But, he also knew, just as we must learn, that we are not supposed to go out on a walk trying to *make it* a "deep" and beautiful experience. Doing that makes it infinitely more difficult to accomplish—it's simply too much pressure. The feelings of peace, connection, and awareness of God, come naturally while walking in your own direction and pace—and in thinking *your* own thoughts, whatever they may be.

Perhaps you have just had and argument with someone and are fuming about it, or maybe thoughts about yard work reign supreme. Any of a million things rush in and out of consciousness on a walk, or one nagging concern can chew at the heart. What is amazing is walking's ability to transform consciousness regardless of effort. Surprising insights seem to jump into the frame. Peace creeps in, the focus widens, and it all seems spontaneous and quite apart from mental strain. It's a bit miraculous really, a bit wonderful, and, surprisingly a bit of a secret from the common man, little used, and under appreciated.

Even more miraculous, you will find that, after time, here and there a silence overtakes, and you begin to open to even greater feelings, and to the ability to hear the "thousand voices praising God," one of which will be yours.

What is important on these walks is not to force your mind in any direction. Just let it go. It is also important to do this alone, if at all possible. This is your walk. If you must take children with you, make sure they are in a stroller or wagon (I use two radio flier wagons tied together with a kid in each) so they will not be talking to you or stopping your pace. However, I strongly advise against sharing your walks with another adult. It will simply be too tempting to talk to each other. Remember, this is not about socializing, but about *you*. As Fredrick Frank put it, "For you can look at things while talking or with a radio going full blast, but you can see only when the chatter stops."

Walk daily, make time to do it—it doesn't have to be more than thirty minutes. I guarantee that after a month you will never want to give it up. Chances are, you will smile more, be more patient, and you will think more clearly. The peace you gain from this simple exercise can give you the beginnings of a new and solid platform from which to rebuild faith and closeness to God, for walking enables a peace and stillness to enter the heart that comes through the act itself. Your ability to be receptive awakens again, much in the way you were in the beginning of your faith. This stillness is extremely valuable. Xhou Xuanjing writes, "The secret of the receptive must be sought in stillness; within stillness there remains the potential for action."

It is not necessary to wait for the right mood to come and energize you into action. You don't have to be "in the mood" to spend time on yourself, or in the mood to walk. As a matter of fact, there will probably be many days when you are not. The familiar adage "old habits die hard" is especially true in this case. That is why it is important not to rely on mood to galvanize you into action.

Mood lies. Mood says, "Oh, I am too busy today washing windows to spend time reading," or "My husband will think I am a bad wife if I take this hour to myself..." Mood says, "I am tired," or depressed or generally "not in the mood" to go for a walk. Mood saps your resolve to change just as it can drive your initial desire *to* change. It is for this reason, its variable nature, that mood, like the dieter's nemesis, "willpower" must not be relied upon.

Pearl Buck said, "I don't wait for moods. You accomplish nothing if you do that. Your mind must know it has to get down to work." She is right.

It is absolutely important to resolve to "just do it," to make taking time for yourself a life habit, that, like prayers, is close to inviolate. Once you start you will never want to return to that empty shell that was yourself.

It is highly likely that those closest to you will resist the time you are spending on yourself, and the time you take for your walks. Just remember that this is a natural response to change. Knowing that resistance to change is natural is the key to weathering the comments and negativity you might experience from those closest to you. It is your best defense.

Beginning

In my case, my passion is writing, so every morning I began writing. One of those first mornings, my husband (usually a very supportive person) lost his hairbrush, and noticed me writing at the table. He walked up to me and said, rather snidely, "Oh, don't worry about *me*, just go back to your writing."—expressing his frustration in a way he never would have if I had I been doing a task he was used to. He would hardly have said, had I been washing the dishes, for example, "*Fine*, you just go back to your *dishes*!"

If I didn't expect this kind of resistance as natural, I might have taken it to my heart ("Oh, I am a bad wife...") and stopped writing. Instead, I shrugged it off (with some effort, I admit!), seeing it for what it was, a natural response. I located the brush with my home inventory locator-map that my husband assumes I possess, and returned to my writing.

If you know to expect resistance, and recognize it for what it is—not an attack against you or what you are doing, but a natural resistance to change, you can smile to yourself when you see it pop up. As walking and taking "you time" begins to be a part of your normal routine, people in your life will get used to it and cease to be threatened.

You must be strong and resolute, and by all means, *don't* share what you are doing with someone who is in this resistance phase for validation or support. They will very likely try to take the wind out of your sails, even if they are not intentionally calculating or malevolent normally. Don't open yourself up for that. Be secure that what you are doing is leading to an increase of faith, happiness and peace in your life that will ultimately benefit your loved ones as well as yourself.

You are about to embark on a wonderful opportunity for change. Don't wait for the perfect time, mood, or situation to begin—just *begin*. As Kabir, the fifteenth century mystic philosopher said, "Wherever you are is the entry point!"

> *It is not righteousness that ye
> turn your faces towards east or west;
> But it is righteousness—to believe in God
> and the Last Day...*
>
> – Qur'an (2: 177)

> *Deep down in me I knowed it was a lie,
> and He knowed it.
> You can't pray a lie—I found that out.*
>
> – Mark Twain

Chapter Five

Prayer

Prayer is the keystone of Islam. It is said of prayer, "The first matter that the slave will be brought to account for on the Day of Judgment is the prayer. If it is sound, the rest of his deeds will be sound. If it is bad, then the rest of his deeds will be bad (Al-Tabarani)."

Anyone who has been through the experience of being a "new" Muslim knows the joy of prayer—of not being able to wait for the next prayer time to come, of having all of the hairs stand up on the back of your neck while your eyes fill with tears as the *adhan* echoes through the mosque. So, too, anyone who has been in the throws of real despair also knows the strong, urgent, and comforting connection to God that prayer provides during a time of personal tragedy.

When going through a low point in faith, however, a change in prayer can be one of the first indications of a problem.

I have been through that initial high point of faith and practice. I have also been through the low. I know from talking to other Muslims that I am not alone.

One frank and honest sister recently mentioned to me, "God, I remember when I couldn't wait to pray. Now, I do pray…but I don't look forward to it anymore."

The truth is, being at a low point in the practice of prayer is not uncommon. Nor do I believe it is a harbinger of bad character or morality. In fact, I would wager that almost everyone goes through a period of "not really feeling like it," at least inside, even if they are not willing to admit to it.

The symptoms are many—In my case, I would often forget to pray until either the last minute, or would miss the time altogether and have to "make it up." My mind would wander uncontrollably to the point that I would forget which *raka'* I was on. *Fajr* was always missed, and I would actually look forward to getting my period and its accompanying respite from what had become for me, yet another chore.

During this time, guilt was a constant partner in my life. I felt bad, sacrilegious, and like a fake —but I dared not "let on" about the way I was feeling.

All around me, then still an "active" member of the Islamic community, I would see and hear about other people's relationship to prayer and would feel increasingly guilty and inadequate by comparison. I grew hopeless, feeling almost as if I had a secret that no one else shared. I remember one sister in particular, saying how peaceful prayer made her feel—and how it was like "an island of peace" that was her private time between herself and God. At the time, I just looked at her, feeling a mixture of awe and jealousy. She was obviously much "deeper" than me, I thought. In fact, during many prayers, as I once again forgot my place, I would bring her words to mind, and wonder just what had happened to me that had brought me so far away from the ideal.

Another statement that greatly affected me was made during a *halaqa* at a local mosque, where the subject was prayer and the mercy of God.

The *halaqa* had recently been taken over by a new group leader, an imposing woman given to voluminous black veils and armfuls of beautiful gold jewelry. She seemed very knowledgeable, and was, to be frank, a bit intimidating.

Surveying the room, she asked, "Do you think Allah will answer your prayers if you don't pray Fajr? Do you think Allah will be merciful to you?"

Looking around, I noticed several women shaking their heads in the negative.

The group leader went on, "That's right, no!" "Allah will not answer your prayers if you don't pray Fajr." "Do you expect Allah to be merciful if you don't offer your prayers correctly?"

I remember looking around at all of those glowing faces, secure in the knowledge that they were praying at the appropriate level of perfection, while I, sitting there properly "*hijabed* and *jilbabed*," the very picture of Islamic goodness, was really a terrible fraud, and a failure as a Muslim.

In addition to having guilt as a constant companion, I now added fear. Fully believing what this *halaqa* leader said about the mercy of God, I became extremely afraid. I already knew my prayers were horribly lacking, but I was in a slump that I simply could not pull myself out of.

Now that I knew God would not help me, I felt hopeless.

Filled with this guilt, fear, and a sense of disconnection with God (after all, he was "angry" with me wasn't he?), I began to approach prayer with a sense of inevitable doom and judgment that only served to magnify my alienation to an even higher degree.

As it often happens in life, bad turned to worse. I began to experience a string of personal tragedies. In a short amount of time, my family and I suffered from a miscarriage, the imprisonment of my sister, the possibility that my son might be suffering from Autism, and the death of my husband's brother.

My worst fears began to be realized as I felt God's wrath upon me. Worse yet, I worried that, although I constantly beseeched God for help and relief, he would not answer my call because my prayers, as well as myself, were not perfect.

In the midst of despair, I turned to some members of the Islamic community for emotional support, only to have my faults magnified back to me a hundred fold. One woman even said, "It is no wonder you had a miscarriage," meaning it had been a sign and punishment from God.

I finally completely broke down.

I, the former example of "excellent Islamic womanhood," one always called on to introduce and acquaint new people with Islam and the community, dropped out of everything, went on tranquilizers, and ran home to my family.

It was there, with my non-Muslim family, and surrounded by non-believers in a very small country town, that I began my first return to solitude.

I would go for long walks, oblivious to the startled stares of passers-by. I was in such emotional pain that other people's reactions to me no longer mattered. I also began to read again—not books on "the punishments of hell," or the merits of *hijab*, but my old, battered Qur'an, one of the few things I took with me.

There, in the midst of my lowest point, I began to notice the "non-gloom and doom" portions of the Qur'an—a side of Islam and God that I, and I realized, many other Muslims around me in our well-meaning zeal, had forgotten.

The realization gradually dawned on me that, while it was good to focus on the wrath of God and ideal practice, the focus had become oddly skewed toward those themes to the exclusion of all else. In isolation I was able to step back and see what had, in the beginning, been so clear (a period when I also had time to myself), that God *really was* literally Most Gracious, Most Merciful. It was no one's right to assail or limit that fact.

I began to realize that the books I read, the company I kept, and the beliefs I let into my heart during the years of my declining faith had been geared less toward my relationship with God than my need to seek validation in the path I had chosen.

Although no one can argue with the assertion that a focus on the right practice of religion in all of its aspects—from prayer, to behavior, and even dress is an important and indispensable part of Islam, there comes a point, where practices can become both exclusive and exclusionary rather than worship. Instead, they become a mark of belonging, and the realm of appearances can begin to take on a dangerously significant importance.

If I had only been honest enough, like the woman who shared her feelings with me, to admit to how I was feeling about prayer, I might have realized that I wasn't the first or the last Muslim to feel that way. I may have even found someone who had gone through it themselves, and found a way to recover from the same slump. Maybe they could have told me, before I had to learn it the hard way, that in trying so hard to keep up appearances, and in trying to belong, I had forgotten the role of the *self*— of the importance of bringing the "me" to prayer. The conviction that prayer was between myself and God was honestly missing—and no amount of belonging or acceptance in a group—no matter how "Islamic" it appeared or even *was* could ever replace that fact.

Again and again, I read from the opening chapter of the Qur'an, "Thee do we worship, And Thine aid we seek," and realized I *could*, in fact, must seek the help of God as both my duty, and my right. This was a fact that no one could (or should try) to take away.

It was ironic that how I felt about the imperfection of my prayers, both as a result of my own beliefs, and as a result of the comments and lessons from other Muslims, the very lessons and beliefs that were supposed to prompt me to improve my prayer, in fact only served to increase my alienation. I was approaching prayer in the belief that I was so bad, that my prayers were so far from some lofty ideal, that God would never listen to me or offer help.

In my long and solitary walks, in the midst of my self-imposed seclusion from the "community," I began to gain a new perspective on how I interacted with other Muslims—as well as my motivations for doing so. I admitted that, more than anything else, in the last few years, all of the talk, activities, and efforts to "belong" in the Muslim community, all of the effort that had supposedly been about God, had a great deal more to do with appearances and "fitting in." In this reality, there was little wonder that my prayer suffered.

The rather surprising and *nice* thing about my realization was that, like turning on the light after a nightmare, being honest about what my "Islamic experience" had degenerated into, marked the beginning of clarity, and actual optimism.

I went home and instigated some changes.

First, I stepped back from the "community."

This may seem a bit strange, and even "sacrilegious," but for me it was absolutely necessary. I knew that the community was good (in theory) and ultimately important, but for me it had become a quest to "belong," and as such had put a wall between myself and real faith.

Unfortunately, guilt proved to be a major obstacle against this step. After all, I worried, aren't we all responsible for building the Islamic community? If we all start dropping out, how will any good be accomplished? After much thought, I ultimately decided that the answer had to be found in the oft-repeated phrase, "first help yourself—only then can you help others."

Second, I made the conscious decision to go back and discover my real self again. As trite as that sounds, it was quite necessary. I accomplished this by simply doing what I loved, writing, and taking turns around my neighborhood in my trusty Keds. Simplistic? Yes, it was, but the neat thing about it was it worked.

I now understood that I hadn't been bringing my real self and heart to my religion. I buried that self in a million affectations that I thought were better than what I actually was. As a result, there was no hope, no possibility for real faith or a strong connection to God. My public performance of faith surely shined by all outward measures, yet, inside it smacked of a hollowness that eventually ate at my soul.

Third, I had to resolve to show up at prayer.

This meant that I had to simply pray. I didn't approach it negatively, worried about my "feelings." I didn't think about God being "angry" with me, and instead constantly recalled to mind "Most Gracious, Most Merciful." I decided to take the Quranic requirement, "establish regular prayers," quite literally. Along with consciously tossing the complex feelings I had about prayer. I simply had to "show up" to pray, committed to the quantity. Strangely, the quality began to grow as I came back to myself.

Finally, I began to do some things to encourage myself. Although these things are different for every person, for me it simply consists of doing "tricks" that put me in a prayerful mood.

First, I made a list of verses from the Qur'an that stirred my heart and gave me hope. They could be any verse that seemed to "speak to me." What was important was that the list was private and of my exclusive choosing. This step had the nice fringe benefit of recharging my genuine interest in the Qur'an.

Creative by nature (I am so right-brained my head leans to the side), I went all out, using beautiful paper, calligraphy pens, and even framed some.

Another trick I used was making my own special place in my home where I could pray—it's not particularly grand, actually a just a corner of my dining room. There, I have a gurgling fountain, a soft, and fragrant prayer rug (Ah, the many wonders of *Bounce*), and a completely toy and clutter free atmosphere. It is a tiny place really, no more than three feet by five, but the carpeting, seldom trod upon in that spot, is still plush and thick. It is an area that gives me, albeit, not quite, Virginia Wolf's ideal "Room of One's Own," but an island of serenity that is mine, nonetheless.

The idea of a "special place" may seem silly, but the respite it provides from visual distraction, clutter, paperwork, toys, and all of the emotional distractions they evoke, as well as the added dimension of focus and meaning that creeps back into the prayer itself, well outstrips its intrinsic *hokeyness* factor. Further, I believe this is the very essence behind the famous *hadith,* paraphrased, "the best mosques for women are the inner parts of their houses." Unlike the popular (male) interpretation, that it is meant to discourage women from mosque attendance, I believe that many women are more *privately* spiritual, and, for us, the *best* connection between the soul and God is the one made in solitude.

I also began to keep a prayer outfit, the simple cotton two-piece skirt and scarf that covers everything necessary for prayer. Keeping it in my prayer area affords me respite from the hassle of having to find something suitable to wear when prayer time comes around. Further, having clothes exclusively designated for prayer helps me to "switch gears" into a more spiritual state of mind.

The last trick is my favorite. It involves praying outside during warm nights.

There is something special about being outside, under the night sky, or in a warm breeze, that lends itself to a feeling of closeness to God. A warm summer or fall night, alone, free of noise, conversation, and lights can rival the greatest mosque in its ability to evoke feelings of true faith.

As simple as it sounds, praying outside has become quite rare in modern life, and the opportunity, one Muslims in former years took as a matter of course, has become lost to many of us. The wonderful thing, however, is that it is also one of the many experiences life has to offer that we can simply decide to do. It is only a matter of moving out of the fog of habit, stepping outside, looking up, and saying, "Oh, yeah…" "*That's what the stars look like!*"

A note of caution, should you decide to try any of these methods, or any of your own division. Use a ruthless selection process when deciding to share what you are doing with others. Essentially everything should be experiences of solitude, geared toward the self, not the group. Although nothing in these experiences are "secret," one runs the risk of encountering, at the very least, playful teasing, or at the worst, out and out criticism for embarking on any endeavor of self-improvement.

Unfortunately, it is often those closest to us that are eventually our most active saboteurs. This is not due to a lack of love or care, quite the contrary. In fact, often this negativity is subconscious and even more often veiled. They may say things like, "Why are you doing *that*?" "You are acting so *strange* lately," or any other of the myriad of comments designed to let the wind out of our sails, and maintain the *status quo*.

As I mentioned before, resistance to change is a powerful human trait. It is necessary to be both protective of yourself, and, at the same time, understanding of friends and loved ones.

Not sharing ones "tricks" or the reasons for doing them is probably wise, unless you are confident that you will be supported. When in doubt, keep it to yourself. Upon reflection, you will usually find the real motivations for sharing them are for validation anyway. Ultimately the only validation we really need comes from within.

*...For He knows well the secrets of all hearts...
He is the one that accepts repentance from his servants
and forgives sins: And he knows all that ye do.*

– Qur'an (42: 24-25)

*To make no mistake is not in the power of man;
But from their errors and mistakes;
the wise and good learn wisdom for the future.*

– Plutarch

Chapter Six

Sin and Despair

Ah, the days of innocence.

I'm sure you recall either that period of time soon after you "became a Muslim," or, if you grew up in Islam, those days of youth when, although you may have committed a sin or two, they weren't very serious.

I remember feeling so sure about my good standing with God that I absolutely had no fear of death. I can also remember listening to messages against the various vises of sin with smug enjoyment (perhaps a sin in itself!) congratulating myself that I was not among that group of transgressors.

I recall a conversation that I had with an older woman during that time in my life that held a similar conviction. She believed that she had, heretofore, retained a relatively smudge-free record in the sin department.

She was an American-Muslim, and had converted to Islam approximately eleven years before, after marrying her husband.

She said, "I don't worry about dying. You see, you are forgiven for all your sins as a non-believer the moment you accept Islam. It's my husband I worry about (who had a Muslim upbringing) because we lived together before we got married (she converted after this) and he *is* responsible."

What was remarkable to me about this story *then* and what continues to be remarkable *now* are two different things.

Then, I recall thinking how shocking it was that a Muslim would *knowingly* commit such a huge sin as her husband had. I remember looking at him in an entirely different light after she shared this part of their history with me.

Now, years later, and with a considerably larger block of life-experience behind me, perhaps unfortunately, *his* part of the story no longer holds any surprise. What strikes me now is his wife's ability to remain, in her opinion anyway, relatively free of serious sin.

Sin and Despair

The months before my emotional breakdown and subsequent self-retreat, I was, as I mentioned earlier, at the lowest point in my faith, life and religious practice, a point so low that I earnestly hope and pray never to see its like again.

Unlike the woman I just mentioned, I was not so sure of my good standing with God. Unlike her, my conduct had not always been exemplary in the years since accepting Islam. In fact, I increasingly found myself positively terrified of death and of God.

To me, my sins were innumerable (I was, and probably still am, accurate in that assessment), and, to be honest, were probably a major component in the coinciding downhill slide of my prayers. After all, I already believed God wouldn't listen to or answer my prayers, and on top of that, I was a sinner. What chance did I have?

I now believe that my sins themselves were less of a component in my downward slide than my *attitude* about them. For, like my attitude toward every other aspect of my life as a Muslim, I had departed from my initial authentic connection and focus toward God, and had slowly replaced it with a concentration and focus on the "Islamic Community."

In hindsight, my transfer of concentration seems obvious—yet, the actual process was so slow and gradual, my motives so mixed and self-deceptive, and my mind in such a state of spiritual vulnerability, that I never even noticed that it was happening.

Young, naive, and fully believing that all Muslims were good and followed Islam to the letter, I trustingly plunged into the influence of every "established" (which meant anyone who had been Muslim longer than me) Muslim I met.

As my attendance in "mosque life" became more regular, including *halaqas*, gatherings, and individual friendships, I, like countless others, struggled to learn the intricacies of behavior and knowledge that would help me fit in to the new world I had chosen to be a part of.

The quest to belong is a powerful one, and my desire to never again hear the words, "No, dear, *this* is how you do it," or any other similar correction was strong. I just wanted to be a Muslim, something I began to believe was a lot more complicated than saying "*La illaha ill Allah.*"

As anyone who has been in this situation knows, a real and serious vulnerability goes hand in hand with a desire to learn something new. The very nature of the student is vulnerability. When the mind is open to others for example and instruction it is all too easy for the bad to come in with the good.

In my quest to belong in the community, I was unsure and impressionable. So impressionable, in fact, that any comment, earnest or passing, would go straight to my heart like a piercing arrow. If someone said, "Oh, dear, you know Muslims don't keep pictures in their houses," I would flush red with embarrassment and hide away my photos ever after, whether I understood the reasoning behind it, and was convinced by that reasoning or not. It was enough that something was said and done by the women around me to make it "gospel truth," never mind if the logic behind it was sound.

I wanted to fit in, and be a "good Muslim," like I believed everyone else was. It was this attitude that changed my feelings about sin.

I remember my second visit to the mosque clearly.

The same woman who so kindly and openly met me on my first venture into the mosque agreed to accompany me and introduce me to the Friday *halaqa* group.

In the weeks previous, I had corresponded with her through the mail, asking her innumerable questions about Islam and Muslims. I also confided in her about the young Palestinian man I had recently met and was beginning a relationship with.

Like yesterday, I can feel the soft carpet under my feet as I ascended the staircase with her to the woman's section of the mosque. As we reached the top, she put her hand on my shoulder and said, "Oh, Lynn, by the way, don't mention the fact that you have a boyfriend to the women here tonight. It would *not* be understood."

This became my first experience with shame as a Muslim, shame that something I was doing was "wrong," but, even more pressing, that the thing *itself* wasn't as important as the imperative of *not revealing it* to the Muslims around me, Muslims who would presumably, in their comparative innocence, be boundlessly shocked.

Shame is a powerful force in the Islamic world. Essentially, shame is fear—fear of what others might think or say about us. I believe from my years spent entrenched in the community, that shame reigns supreme in a realm where, presumably, guilt once stood.

Guilt, when felt in force, is powerful, and ultimately *positive*. It is intensely private and ultimately the catalyst that leads to change. Guilt is the small voice of conscience that tells us we shouldn't be doing something, or shouldn't *have* done something. It is a gift from God—our own internal map to help us find "the straight way."

It is guilt that nags at me when I have engaged in an afternoon of gossip. Guilt haunts me with past wrong deeds—wrongs I have committed against others as well as myself. And guilt prompts me to say to myself, "In the future, for God's sake, I won't do *that* again!" Guilt needles me again and again until I actually do follow through on that vow.

Shame is something entirely different. Shame only requires me to *hide* my sins. As long as I can conceal my faults from others I don't have to feel, deal with, or learn from them. It is a destructive force, the originator of falsehood, and, like taking an aspirin to ease the pain of a headache, shame dulls the pangs of a guilty conscience by offering the soothing balm of the ability to say *I belong*.

The whispering voice of shame is what I listened to when I wore my biggest scarf and blackest *jilbab*, removed my fingernail polish and toned down my makeup to the point of undetectability when I attended *halaqas* or community events. Shame prompted me to turn down the volume on my car stereo as I turned into the mosque parking lot.

In short, shame prompts me to do things that make me look "better" than I feel I am, and say things I really don't have conviction for in my heart. It is the ultimate impetus of doing something "to be seen of men," and is the heart and soul of hypocrisy—a wall between the individual and God. Ultimately the effect of shame on faith is like water on a fire.

Virginia Woolf said, "If you can't tell the truth about yourself, you can't tell it about other people."

Unfortunately, the woman who advised me to keep my boyfriend to myself didn't realize the message behind this statement. Too mired by years in the culture of shame in her community of Muslims, she didn't understand that she was laying the foundation for my introduction to it, for the keystone holding the culture of shame in place is self-secrecy, and the resulting belief that we alone are imperfect. After all, if you can't share "I'm going through this...", how can you ever hear, "Oh, yeah, I've been there...Here's how I worked through it."

The result of years in this atmosphere was that I was a model of Islamic propriety on the outside. I fit in perfectly. I had mastered the ins and outs of "mosque behavior" with the best of them.

On the inside, I didn't feel so perfect. In fact, I increasingly felt like a fraud. I felt terrified that someone might find me out, and uncover my many and varied faults—perhaps discover that (for starters) I liked listening to music, almost always prayed *Fajr* late, occasionally ate Rice Crispy Treats even though I *knew* they were made with gelatin, and that, although I was an avid proponent of *hijab*, inside I didn't always believe it was such a good idea.

It's not that I was blithely unaware of the glaring differences between my outward projection of myself, and my inward reality; quite the opposite. I was all too aware of my hypocrisy, a knowledge that began to cloud my perception of everything else around me. Everything and everyone began to smack of hollowness and superficiality, from the women at the mosque, to the Islamic community at large, to even Islam itself. I became increasingly depressed, wondering, "what's the point?"

Instead of dropping out of everything to re-examine my involvement and motives, however, I continued, driven by the ever-powerful need to belong. After all, I had worked hard to become a respected and accepted member of the community, a community that all of my friends, and everyone I knew, was a part of. If I left, where would I be? Who would I know? I would be a nobody among the unbelievers.

I didn't realize the ironic truth that I had paid a high price for belonging within the Islamic community (and notice I use the word belonging, not *being*)—a price I paid with the sale of my authentic self and my relationship with God.

It seems both ridiculous and horrible, but I had replaced God with the community. I cared more about what *they* thought of me than God.

What seems so clear in hindsight was deceptively illusive to me then. Although I knew "Islam" was a word that was growing increasingly meaningless to me, I couldn't really pinpoint why. All I did knew was that the lower I sunk in faith, the less convinced I became in what I was doing, the less I wanted to pray, and the more shame and fear I felt.

I knew God was angry with me. I just knew it. I feared death more than ever. But my fear of the community was even greater. I knew how I would fare if "the truth" about me got out. I knew I would be talked about, ridiculed, and ultimately rejected—I would be *judged*. Worse, the reason I knew this would happen was because I *was* the community, *I* had done this myself to other people who didn't meet the standard of the "ideal Muslim." I knew what to expect and tried to support the façade I had erected at all costs.

It was at this time, in a moment of weakness, that I confided my feelings about prayer, *hijab*, and personal problems I was having, to a group of friends, who reacted with a ferocity of judgment and recrimination that, both sent me reeling, and reinforced my fears.

Soon after, when the string of difficult events that I referred to earlier began to occur—the combination beat me into the retreat that both sent me home and jettisoned me out of the community.

It was there, in the time alone and in its absence, I began to see the role the community had come to play in my life, how what I had allowed it to become had eclipsed a once strong practice of Islam and made it into a pitiful shadow of what it had been.

First, I replaced my previous healthy sense of guilt with shame about my transgressions and shortcomings, and in so doing translated the whole meaning of sin into something quite different—from a thing between me and God to a thing between me and people. It seems so obvious now, but the transfer was such a gradual process, my motives so unclear and unexamined, and the community was such an easy substitute, that I didn't realize what I was doing.

Second, I had given my self-image, power, and personal integrity away to that group of individuals that made up my community. I had lost my ability to think for myself. Who was I after all? This ultimately resulted in a horrible and nagging fear of recrimination and judgment.

I remember being so distraught after the horrified reaction of my "friends" to my imperfections and experiences, that I would lie in bed physically sick with worry, stung by their judgment and fearful of their ability to share their knowledge of my "true self" to the community at large.

It was when I returned home that I first realized the role, and the misplaced power I had given people over my life and self-perception.

Like an abusive relationship, the outsider often looks in and wonders, "My God!" "Why does she stay?" "She should just leave the lout!" while the abused woman hangs on, affected by every word and opinion of her partner, not realizing the power she has given away in a stage of love that passed long ago. I needed an outsider, a disinterested and uninvolved party to point out the obvious.

Thank God, my identical twin sister, a person genuinely interested in my well-being, stepped into this role.

I sat in my mother's living room in a cloud of grief from the string of personal setbacks, and despair over the judgment heaped upon my head from the people I had been closest to. My son was playing at my feet, and the phone rang.

When I heard my sister's voice I broke down. In a torrent of grief I told her everything that had been happening. I mentioned that my friends had told me that I was suffering the judgment of God, I was headed to hell, and that I was worried I wouldn't be accepted anymore. On and on I went until she said, "Hold on! Who are they to say what God is doing or thinking about you?! And who are they to say you are going to hell?" "Why have you given them so much power over how you feel? "They are just women!"

With that, it was like a light bulb turned on. For the first time, I had opened a window to a voice *outside* the house of belonging I had built around myself. That voice told me I could open the door and walk out. It was a simple idea, but an idea that needed an outsider to give it voice nonetheless.

For the first time, the notion, that some of the people in the Muslim community—their thoughts and opinions, actions and motives might not be synonymous with Islam occurred to me. In fact, they could never be synonymous, no matter how ideal or well intentioned they may be. Even more important, I realized that to think or accept that they know how God will judge someone or show his mercy was a mistake—both in them, and in me.

More than just a trite recitation of the maxim, "It doesn't matter what people think of you," I realized, *really* realized, that I didn't need anybody's approval or even membership in the "community" to be a Muslim. True faith must be between myself and God alone. The approval of God was the only thing I needed. Simple as that sounds, the re-discovery of that fact was an instant simplification and immense relief.

This new perspective allowed for a complete transformation in the level of fear I harbored in my attitude toward sin, and admitted new hope and a sense of possibility. After all, if I didn't have to seek approval from people, then I was absolutely free to leave all of my focus toward God, where it should have always remained. Had I not been so distracted by my quest to develop an "Islamic identity," it would never have strayed to such a poor shadow of a substitute in the first place.

With this, an immense weight lifted off of my shoulders, and the world literally opened up to me. Even the colors seemed brighter and more vibrant. I began to read my Qur'an, searching for all of the references to sin. Like a gift from God, I came across the most beautiful (and comforting) verse, "Say: 'O my servants who have transgressed against their souls! Despair not of the mercy of God: For God forgives all sins: For He is Oft Forgiving, Most Merciful (39: 53)."

I must have read this verse a dozen times before, but then, immersed in my self-righteous fog, when I firmly believed that I was doing everything absolutely right in life, I had paid no particular notice. In fact, I blithely overlooked it. Now, as I read the verse, I felt sense of restoration, and of hope. I felt that, God was not "against me," that He would be merciful to me if I would only change and refocus back to "the straight way."

I also began to have a sense that the perfection that I had come to expect form myself, and from every other Muslim, was not reasonable or even possible. Mistakes will be made. We are human after all, and we, unlike the angels, are not perfect.

Although, I didn't jump to the other extreme and begin to believe that our inherent fallibility gives us free license for sin, nor that one should ever be secure in the eventuality of forgiveness, I realized that there has to be a happy medium between the "sin and ask forgiveness later" mindset, and the rigid, strangely gleeful "burn-in-hell" mentality that seems to hold such popularity in Islamic circles.

I did not come to the conclusion that the Islamic community is bad in itself, or that it should be rejected entirely, on the contrary. I believe the community is necessary, worthy and good when made up of personally secure people of integrity, knowledge, and understanding. But, I *do* feel it can be a dangerous place for many new, or by nature impressionable people, simply because the urge to belong and conform to outside expectations, especially when those "others" are people one respects and wishes to emulate, is so strong.

Although it is good to emulate worthy people, it is quite possible (and probable) to come to the community unprepared, as I believe many "new Muslims" are, to distinguish the worthy from the unworthy. It is also possible for a "good person" to be so good as to be unauthentic (I know because I once filled this role), and set an impossibly high example to follow—an example that only dooms the newcomer to failure and faith-crushing frustration.

It cannot be denied that, for many people in Islamic communities, the definition of sin has become oddly skewed. This is also dangerous for the newcomer, because it warps the ability to accept the capacity of God to be forgiving.

The Qur'an specifically says that sin is against our own souls, to our own detriment. If one's energy is excessively focused toward the group, and finding a place within it, it is all too easy to completely lose the ability to view sin (and deal with it) as a personal struggle.

The Qur'anic meaning of sin as personal is not only the remedy for shame and the pathway to constructive guilt and conscience, but it is also a doorway to the mercy and hope of God. It offers freedom from the constraints of people-pleasing, and leaves the real relationship between the self and God to flourish.

I don't believe it is necessary to have a personal crisis in order to change this focus. But it is necessary, when lost in the grip of shame and fear of outside recrimination, to step back from "community involvement" for at least a short time.

For many people this idea sounds a little scary, especially if "belonging" is an important motivator (as it was for me, and I suspect is for most people). Of course, fitting in and having friends is fun. There is nothing wrong with that. However, if you find yourself, as I did, paying a price for this "fitting in," a price that includes behaving, and speaking in a way that doesn't always correspond with your inner heart and private behavior—in effect hiding certain parts of yourself in order to be accepted, you are probably paying a higher price than you think. Chances are, most people who find themselves in this situation, have unknowingly replaced *people* as a center of being, and have seen their inner self-images as well as their relationship to private devotion plummet.

Once you realize that you are, in fact, concretely mired within this category, it is surprisingly simple to get back on the right track again. The only difficulty is coming to the point when one not only recognizes the problem, but is also bothered by it enough that unease outweighs the emotional high that goes with acceptance. When that point comes there

Sin and Despair

are very simple steps that help a great deal, and, although I believe that each person has an internal sense of "the right way," here are some suggestions that can help:

- Take a step back from the community. This includes both "community involvement" and social obligations.

    If this is hard for you, give it a set time period. I suggest three months. Stating a time period will both help you, if you are a particularly social person, and will give you a time period you can present to others.

- Expect resistance.

    You will get numerous phone calls and invitations during this time to *haliqas*, fundraisers, parties, etc. Resist them! Calmly, resolutely, and politely say, "I am spending my energies on some time alone for three months, so I won't be accepting any invitations for a while." If this is difficult for you, and you have a hard time saying no (as many women do), let the answering machine pick up.

- Don't worry that you will lose all of your friends or contacts in the community.

    This is simply a "playground mentality" nagging at you. They will be there when you come back. And, if they really can't accept or understand your need for time away, consider the possibility that they are not people you will genuinely miss knowing.

- Limit your social contacts to those people you can really be yourself around.

    I find a good rule of thumb is, if I don't completely stress about tidying the house before a person visits my home, they generally fall into this category!

    Don't be surprised if your list of really close friends is actually very small (or even nonexistent!). When I did this I found I only had two, and one of them was my sister.

- Limit social obligations, or better yet, eliminate them.

    Often, for Muslim women, there is a never ending string of obligations. We accept them all, from a fundraising dinner to babysitting for friends. Although it is good to help out when you can, in our communities, it is all too easy to be overwhelmed by requests on our time and energies. There are times in our lives when we have to focus on ourselves to be healthy, emotionally, spiritually and physically.

If you feel guilty about stepping back from obligations, remember that it is only for a short period. In most cases, someone else could do the job as well as you, and, if you say, "I can't" to someone they will eventually move on to the next person on their list.

- Practice saying, "No, I really can't right now."

For many Muslim women, "no" is the least used word in their vocabulary—it may take some time to shake the dust off. I suggest writing a "no sentence" on a piece of paper next to the telephone, or, better yet, let the machine take care of it. Remember, if someone persists in trying to convince you of something after you have refused, they are crossing your boundaries. The only way to avoid that nagging feeling of being taken advantage of that so many of us experience, is by finally deciding that "no" is a fence that cannot be jumped. Like with children, if you say no, and are later swayed by entreaty (over something trivial), the no simply becomes a prompt for negotiation. It is the same with adults! When your "no" means no, you will create a boundary that can never be crossed. It does take a few times, however, for people who are used to negotiating with you, that you really mean business. Persevere, try it, and you will find you spend a lot less time being *convinced* of things, and feeling taken advantage of—and far less likely to cringe when the telephone rings. The increase in self-respect you feel will be truly surprising.

- Walk regularly and do the things you love.

If you are not doing these things to re-awaken your authentic self, it will be next to impossible to discard your outward focus toward sin and shame. Remember the great prophets Abraham, Jesus, and Muhammad all had periods of solitary reflection in their lives. If we can strive to emulate them in other areas, certainly we can take their example in this one as well!

- Write on a piece of paper, chalkboard, or message board, whatever can remain for a long period of time and can be in view in your most oft-occupied space, "This is between me and God."

Whenever you glance at this sentence, you will be reminding yourself (and others in the household), of what you are doing, and the merit of it!

He knows what is before them
And what is behind them:
And to God go back all questions (for decision).
– Qur'an (22: 76)

Take away the cause, and the effect ceases.
– Miguel de Cervantes

Chapter Seven

Rethinking Sin

Nobody likes to think about sin—that is, unless it is *someone else's*. Even when we do think about our own sins—past and present, it is with a fleeting cringe that we hasten past. We strive to slam the door as fast and as firmly as possible on the feelings that reflections on sin evoke, feelings of shame, fear, guilt, even embarrassment. Sometimes, we even avoid thinking about a particular sin too much, lest we become driven to *stop* doing it. There is another way of looking at sin, however, a way that is significantly less painful, and infinitely more constructive.

Instead of hastening past the door where we try to hide and forget our sins, we can peek in—just a bit. We can even pull out one or two, and consider the fact that we have squirreled them away there in the first place. To have done that, we must have decided somewhere along the line that whatever has been done, or is still being done, is negative. That, in itself, constitutes a step of learning. With that realization, we can then ask the question, Would I do it again? If the answer is no, a resounding "No!" felt in the depths of your heart, you have learned from that sin, and, if you have earnestly asked for forgiveness from God, repented. If, on the other hand, your heart's answer is "I am still doing that thing," or "I may continue to do that thing in the future," you have not yet learned whatever lesson it is you have to learn.

A way of thinking about sin is that it is actually a weakness that holds a particular pull or attraction, an attraction that makes moving on from it particularly difficult. Many people consider this to be the real work of life—the impediment that blocks genuine peace and closeness to God.

Once you begin to quiet the outside chatter, and make room in your life for the real work to begin again, you can explore the reasons why. You can, through an honest acceptance and appraisal of your "temptations," begin to heal them.

Rethinking Sin

Perhaps you promise yourself over and over that you will never backbite again, yet can't seem to stop yourself at the next juicy opportunity. Maybe you miss prayers, lie, are unkind and impatient, or don't give enough charity. Maybe you are even having an extramarital affair (yes, it does happen, and if it *is* you, you will neither be the first nor the last).

Whatever the vice, and they are innumerable in possibility, it is important to realize that, whatever the sin, there is a very personal reason and impetus, a real driving force within that is, for you, a particular weakness. If you can identify the weakness, you can work to change it, heal that part of you that is askew, and never return to that sin, really the behavioral symptom of a "disease in the heart" that you must heal.

It is far more constructive (and inspiring), to consider sin as an opportunity to work toward change. After all, it is encouraging to know that all of the effort, desire, and intention involved in an honest attempt toward real change is blessed by God.

Working on personal sin is a private endeavor. Contrary to popular opinion (really a legacy of a Western cultural upbringing), it isn't a good idea to share too much in the area of sin. This is between you and God. Keeping it private not only insures against a shift in focus away from God, but it also protects from the very real and unfortunate probability of gossip.

Although "working" on sin can involve everything from prayer to meditation, the simple tool of writing is extremely useful—and one of the best ways to utilize the cathartic power of writing is the time-honored journal.

A journal can be anything, even a notebook, as long as it is kept in a private place, and for your eyes only. Use it to write whatever thoughts come to your mind and seem important. Don't worry about spelling, grammar, or penmanship. This is a private endeavor. If you find yourself stifled by fear of it coming into the hands of your more curious and boundary deficient family members, burn the pages after you are finished writing them. You are not writing for posterity, but only as an aid in thinking, for writing has a surprisingly effective ability to help work through uncertain and muddled thoughts. It helps us come to conclusions and realizations that somehow don't come together in thought alone.

If you have never been much of a writer this will be a new and wonderful discovery for you, and a tool you can use again and again.

Julia Cameron expresses this idea eloquently in her book, *The Right to Write*, where she says,

> Writing is a spiritual housekeeper.... No matter how secular it may appear, writing is a spiritual tool. We undertake it solo, and not to be facile with puns, it is worth noting that the word does have the word, "soul" embedded in it. Moving alone onto the page, we often find ourselves companioned by higher forces, by a stream of insights and inspirations that seem somehow "other" than our routine thinking.

In addition to writing whatever comes to you, make a list of any bad things you have done in the past, but now know with a certainty that you would never again be tempted to do. Remember this is all private and not meant to be shared (this may be one page you may wish to burn or otherwise destroy).

When you finish writing, one of the most cathartic things you can do is to offer a prayer for forgiveness. With that, you can feel genuinely good knowing you have repented and learned from those mistakes, as well as feel hopeful in the forgiveness of God. You can actually begin to view those mistakes as stepping stones that have marked the way on your journey to who you are today.

In this vein Machaelle Small Wright writes in her book, *Behaving as if the God in All Life Mattered*,

> I offer this search for the spiritual thread in my life as an example for you to use when looking back into your own life. I can't adequately express how each event was built on top of the previous ones, creating a pattern of oneness, wholeness. I saw the light of synthesis. The result has been more and more I don't look back in anger and disappointment—instead, I look, back in gratitude, even celebration.

This is not to suggest that we celebrate our mistakes. As Muslims, we believe sin is a thing to be mourned. But, in looking back over our lists of sins, we can say, "I learned this." We can reconstruct the mistakes and resulting lessons gleaned from those mistakes and see how those lessons have built up to create the person we are today. Listing "repented sins" is a great tool that opens a window into the ways you have been transformed over the years. It also gives you a hint of the path you can continue to take toward "the straight way" during the time you have on this earth.

To move on to the next step, and make a list of unrepented sins, is significantly more difficult, but it is important not to avoid it due to depression or a sense of defeat. After all, if you have a bad feeling about some of the things you are doing now in your life, you are moving in the right direction. Further, writing them down does not make the sin any more real than it already is (as opposed to talking about them), and it also opens up the possibility of using the sword of awareness to write them *down,* and out of your life.

Remember, this too is extremely private. If you know you will share your list with someone else, you will, by nature, self-edit. Leaving something out only shortchanges yourself.

Listing and exploring the *real* reasons behind your desire to commit a particular sin is at the least, illuminating, and at the best, transforming.

The following is an example of this exercise:
1. I backbite

- Reasons:
    I am jealous
    I try to fit in by going along with the conversation
    I am not satisfied with myself
    I am insecure
    I am bored
    I have friends who draw me in
    I am angry

- Possible solutions (free write):

    1. Why am I jealous of that person? Explore this in a journal. Do I feel it gives me more power to tear her down?

    2. Am I around people that backbite a lot? Who are those people? Why am I friends with them? How can I deal with it when they start backbiting?

    3. I am not satisfied with myself. Why am I jealous or insecure about myself? What is missing in my life?

4. How can I get away from boredom (a factor that often plays a part in my temptation to backbite). What positive thing can I start in my life that would give me some joy? What do I love to do? How can I do that?

5. How can I weed through friends? Do I really need to be friends with them? What people bring out the best in me? Who brings out the worst? Who am I happiest with and why?

6. Why am I angry? What is it that is causing me such dissatisfaction and disharmony?

When you begin to understand why you are continually tempted by a stubborn sin, its very temptation seems to weaken. You may even find that, God willing, the next time you are doing whatever it is that you find difficult to change, you will discover the payoff to be significantly less satisfying, perhaps for the first time. In this, like in so many other areas of life, the old cliché is true—knowledge is power. With honest self-knowledge, avoiding sins will become less of a struggle involving willpower, and instead, armed with honest awareness, the appeal of the particular sin simply fades away.

That said, today is a beautiful, sunny day. I look outside, and a gentle breeze beckons. I think it's time to grab a pen and a notebook, head to the swing under the gigantic cedar tree in my backyard, and work on my own list. I, once and for all, must uncover why those Rice-Crispy treats are so darn tempting…

Say to my servants that they should say those things that are best...
– Qur'an (17: 53)

All truths are not to be told
– George Herbert

Chapter Eight
Backbiting and Gossip

Of all of the sins possible on this good earth, I have a sneaking suspicion that backbiting and gossip are probably the most common, as well as the most difficult to curb.

It is often said that backbiting and gossip are women's vices. Although I take issue with this assumption (after all, I have met several men who can hold their own in the gossip department), I do believe gossip has a particular draw for women.

There are innumerable factors that serve to power the virtual "tractor beam" that seems to draw us toward the temptation of gossip. Wide eyed and helpless, we seem to be drawn in again and again, despite our best intentions, and, often solemn, vows of abstinence.

Contributing factors range from jealousy, insecurity and boredom, to a subconscious desire to reinforce our own position within the group. Although these motivators are obvious, and are so close to the surface that their hallmarks are as plainly visible as porcupine quills under the drape of a silk scarf, they are so clouded by the mist of emotion that many of us remain hopelessly unaware of their presence.

I have gossiped with the best of them. In fact, to be completely honest, I still find myself drawn into the temptation on occasion, especially if I am really angry at the moment (a particular weakness of mine).

The truth is, I have had several friendships over the years that, in hindsight, simply *existed* for the purpose of backbiting and gossip. That's all we did when we got together or talked on the telephone. In fact, I remember I had one friend who would begin our conversations with, "So have you heard any gossip lately?"

I'll admit, there were several years in my life when I badmouthed other people with utter abandon and lack of remorse. At the time, I knew

Backbiting and Gossip

"backbiting" was a sin, but somehow just didn't connect it with what I was doing. Negative talk is so social, and lets be honest, it feels so *good* when we are deep in the midst of a juicy gossip fest, that our feelings about it can lie. After all, if it didn't feel good to do it what would be the draw?

When I look back at this particular time in my life, I can see the function backbiting served for me. At the time, when I was an avid and remorseless participant and instigator of what must have been countless hours of gossip, I was a "new community member," still in my "fitting in" stage of belonging to the Islamic community. I was new to *hijab*, new to "mosque life," new to the Muslim "social scene" and new to marriage. I had a stake in convincing both myself, and others, that the rather difficult path I had chosen was the right one, and insecurity fairly oozed out of my pores.

Criticizing those who engaged in actions that didn't represent the ideal of Islamic life I believed I had embarked on, the ideal of Islamic life as I saw it, were fair targets as far as I was concerned. Then, gossip and backbiting simply served the function it has since time immemorial, namely, as a tool to reinforce barriers of belonging and exclusion. For, to say, "Can you believe that she said –or did that?" "I thought that she was such a good Muslim!" serves both to knock someone else down while bringing the speaker's sense of belonging up. "She is like that, therefore I am better than her."—If I can feel superior to another, I can feel more secure in the place I belong.

Later, as I matured a bit, I began to make the connection between what I was doing and the actual sin of backbiting. I wish I could say I completely discovered it on my own, but, like so many other things in life, it took a well-timed comment from another to turn the proverbial light bulb on in my head.

After attending an *Eid* prayer after Ramadan, my family and I were pulling out of a parking space outside. Just then, I spotted an acquaintance I had spoken to inside after the prayer. Walking to her car, she had removed her scarf and *jilbab*, and was now wearing "normal" street clothes. Seeing her, I said, "Look at her, she is such a hypocrite, she was wearing *hijab* inside and now she takes it off!"

Immediately, my brother-in-law turned to me and said, "Oh, so you leave the prayer, come out and backbite someone before you even get out of the parking lot?"

Ouch...But he was right on—and I knew it. In fact, not only was he right on, but, like a bolt of lightning, I realized he was right on for the first time. That moment in the parking lot was the beginning of a change in attitude. For the first time, ridiculous as it sounds now, I really *internally* realized that what I was doing was a sin. It was a message I was finally ready to hear.

I wish I could say I stopped backbiting then and there. I *did* promise myself I would (I can visualize the exact corner we were turning in the parking lot as I silently made that promise). But I didn't.

What I did do, however, was begin to feel the pangs of guilt and conscience for the first time. When I did backbite again (and yes folks, I most certainly did), it no longer held the same guilt-free pleasure. For the first time when I participated in a gossipy conversation, I was aware of what I was doing. I didn't like that feeling.

I began to feel stuck. I would promise myself again and again, usually after gossiping about someone, that I wouldn't do it again. Then, a few days would pass and I would find myself promising again. Like a compulsive over-eater, I would binge on gossip and steep myself in regret afterward. Again, I would promise myself it would be different from then on. The problem was, I was expecting willpower alone to prevent me from my tendency to gossip. I didn't realize that I needed to focus not on the act itself, but on the pull within me that made gossip so tempting in the first place.

After stepping back and spending some time alone, I realized gossip and backbiting had taken on a new function in my life. I noticed that I most often, if not always, would gossip or backbite when I was with a certain group of friends. As I became more and more aware of what I was doing and less comfortable with it, I also began to realize I was not instigating the conversation, but I was participating in it once it began. I would immediately know where the conversation was going, feel momentarily annoyed (just enough to allow me to perch on my moral high-horse), and then would jump in with full participatory gusto.

In my defense, however feeble it may be, I often felt positively horrible during the conversation, and even worse afterward...but for some reason it wasn't enough of an impetus to make me stop. *Why was I doing this?* I often asked myself in genuine bewilderment. After all,

I didn't consider myself a morally weak person in general. Why did I so consistently act in defiance to what I knew and felt to be wrong?

After some serious soul-searching and countless pages of journal writing, I realized I was motivated by three factors.

First, I was worried about being a "good friend." If I didn't participate and validate what my friend was saying, even if it was backbiting against another person, maybe she wouldn't like me anymore. It was a skewed mentality toward friendships that was rearing its ugly head, and it said, "the more friends you have the better...quantity, not quality." "Besides, you don't want to look stuck up and holier-than-thou do you?"

Second, I realized our conversations often drifted into this area out of sheer boredom. When our conversation was lagging, when we had nothing to talk about, our conversations would almost always turn nasty.

Third, I simply didn't know what to say or do to prevent my friends from starting these conversations. Even if I had finally gotten to the point where I (usually) could manage to abstain from *beginning* a gossip session (I had started noticing my own motivators for that), I didn't know how to head my friends off once they began, nor did I know how to gracefully not participate in the conversation.

I did know that the "officially sanctioned method" for stopping gossip was to get up and silently walk out of the room. I didn't have the nerve to do *that* heaven knows. "What? Not play nice? I am a *girl* after all..." I needed to give it some thought. I walked and I wrote, focusing a good deal of my energy on the issue. I wondered what it was about me that was helping to create this problem.

I finally decided that I had to really look at the reason I continued to have a relationship with some of my friends at all.

Lets face it, we have probably all been in the position of having a friend that seems to bring out the worst in us. We find ourselves returning calls, scheduling get-togethers and otherwise interacting with these people out of a sense of duty rather than a genuine wish to do so. Often, after spending a day, or an evening with that person, we find ourselves plagued with a sense of unease about the time, usually spent in gossip, for the simple reason that no other real connection is shared. This is not to say that the other person is bad. It is simply possible for two people to bring out the worst in each other. Sodium and water are peaceful individually, but bring them together and they react violently.

Likewise, it is possible for two people to create a reaction between them that wouldn't be present otherwise. It is also possible for two different people to be at different stages of life. I wouldn't have wanted to be around *myself* five years ago. People learn and evolve at different paces and levels. I didn't even see anything wrong with backbiting in my younger days. I hadn't yet made that connection. Maybe my friend was still there. That doesn't make me better than her, nor does it make her bad. It just means she is still working on that lesson in her life.

I had to decide whether I wanted to continue relationships with people that seemed to result in a problem when we came together. This was a difficult decision for me, both because of my mentality toward friendship, and because of my intense worry about hurt feelings. Regardless, I did break off some relationships, and when I did, I realized, with the clarity of separation, that a few of these relationships provided no enjoyment for me. In fact, I found that I absolutely dreaded ever having to "get together" with them again.

Getting off of my high-horse and realizing that it was quite possible that *they* felt the same way about *me* helped me to say goodbye (and no, I did not call them up and tell them why). I simply did not go out of my way to continue the connection. I would return calls but would be consistently unavailable for meetings, and I would never instigate a call. I found that it wasn't necessary to be rude or hurtful to end a relationship. And I accepted that there is no rule that says I have to be friends with anyone (kindness is another matter). In "our world," where acquaintances can pile up and quickly get out of hand, with telephone messages, invitations and requests for attention accumulating to the point of avalanche, it was a tremendously empowering realization.

The remaining problem was how do deal with the remaining friend that I did want to maintain a relationship with, yet still had a strong tendency to backbite (and I had a strong tendency to join right in). She still had other qualities I really loved in her. What could I do to steer the conversation away from gossip?

I decided I would use three main tactics—I would remain silent, say words like "Oh..." but refrain from participating, adding to, or sustaining with reinforcing remarks, I would try to change the subject as soon as possible, and I resolved to try to say something nice about the person being discussed. After all, I thought, if someone thinks I like an individual, they are less likely to say something negative about them. Further, I decided that it would be a good idea to announce in conversation (although not in the midst of gossip) that I was trying to stop myself from backbiting. I said (truthfully) that I have noticed a problem in myself with backbiting, and have decided to conduct an experiment avoiding it for three months, to see how I do. I asked for support from all of my friends, including reminders should they notice any lapses on my part (this had the nice benefit of making others aware of themselves as well)—this way I had an avenue to playfully accuse others, should they begin to backbite, of "trying to mess up the experiment," a graceful and kind reminder—without focusing on them as the problem.

Of all the methods I found that the last one worked the best. Happily, not only did this work for me, but it seemed to help make my friend more aware of her tendency to backbite. It also had the surprising and pleasant benefit of forcing our relationship to be more meaningful. No longer falling back on the crutch of negative talk, we were free to develop interests and discussions that made our friendship infinitely more positive and satisfying.

Lest I sound too goody-goody and become dishonest, let me reiterate what I touched on earlier. I *do* still find myself backbiting on occasion, usually when I am angry, depressed, or hurt in some way. When I am "down" and at my lowest moments, I am also at my most susceptible to this particular vice. I feel that this is probably true of most sins, and perhaps is the nature of sin itself—the reason sin is often referred to as "a weakness."

It is part of our nature that we, as humans, are never completely cured of our propensity to sin. In fact the temptation to do the wrong thing can be counted to pop up again and again until the grave. Such is the nature of life! However, if we use tools as reminders of the motivations behind the temptation, an exciting thing occurs. Like the wondrous ability of a bedroom light to dissipate the terror of a nightmare, the realization of the motivating forces behind a particular sin can greatly reduce its draw.

There is another side of backbiting that is seldom discussed—namely, how do you deal with it when you find *yourself* the target of backbiting or gossip? When through stupidity, carelessness, or plain old malice, the object of negative talk becomes painfully aware of its existence, especially when that talk comes from the mouths of fellow

Muslims, the effect can be emotionally devastating.

There are few people who haven't been the unfortunate targets of gossip. Nevertheless, when we discover that we are the focus of malicious talk, we react with a mixture of shock, incredulity, and anger. After all, how *dare* they! As creatures used to looking outside of ourselves for a sense of worth and validation, we feel stung to the core. We watch out self-esteem and sense of belonging, at least temporarily, plummet. Worse, when we find that the backbiting has originated in another Muslim, the effect can be even more magnified.

Although most of us have spent several years within the Islamic community, long enough to learn the harsh reality of the product that results from ideal Islam meeting raw human nature, the myth of the "perfect" Muslim hangs on. In fact, not only does the myth hang on, but, for some inexplicable reason, we look for its full manifestation in the lives and practices of those Muslims around us. The frustration and disillusionment that result from this expectation of perfection burn as fiercely and as hot as lava flowing through a cedar forest, and the winds of fury only fan the flames.

Clearly, the only method to stop the destruction created in the wake of this expectation is through the calm, humble acceptance of the simple reality before us—namely, the imperfection of the Islamic community and the individual Muslims that make up that community.

Muslims do some rotten things to each other. When bad things happen at the hands of people that embody the ideals we hold dear, the hurt and shock we experience is immense. Even worse, when it occasionally happens that such malevolence comes from an individual that we respect and expect to behave at an even higher level of perfection than ourselves, say, from a mosque leader, or someone we otherwise perceive as "extremely religious," it can have a profound effect on our morale and confidence in the path we have chosen. For this reason, it is important to have an inner line of defense—a coping mechanism that allows one to weather the occasional assault of words (or actions) that can come our way from sources that personify idealism, our brothers and sisters in Islam.

We often hear the old cliché, "Nobody's perfect." Just as this is true in the general human population, so it is true among Muslims. Yet, in an environment where faith and religious practice hold paramount importance, the hope and idealism harbored within can make this a difficult concept to grasp or even accept. "But....But..." we bluster when we are treated unkindly by another Muslim, or are otherwise witnesses of "un-Islamic behavior." "They are not supposed to act like that!" We not only watch our fellow Muslims drop in our esteem, but feel a sense that Islam itself has somehow been diminished, as if their behavior somehow had the ability to affect its integrity.

The worst thing about the situation is that too many of us find ourselves reeling again and again, stung and shocked each time we find we are the targets of patently un-Islamic behavior, as if it is the very first time we have felt its sting. Like the tormented souls of hell, finding their skins roasted only to have them renewed for the experience again, we feel the pain of betrayal each time a fellow Muslim acts unkindly, recover, and again feel ourselves suffering the very same painful feelings the next time with the freshness of the first.

The question that must be asked is not how we can change the propensity of others, specifically the propensity of Muslims, to act un-Islamically. The question must be, How can we look toward ourselves to change? We must develop a strategy of self-preservation that will allow us to no longer suffer anew each time negativity is aimed our way.

Let us take the example of one of my good friends.

Aimee, an American-Muslim woman, recently divorced from her Palestinian husband of five years. Their divorce was amicable, in fact, an impressive model of the "right" and decent way to end a marriage that just wasn't working out.

Soon after, an acquaintance, widely considered by those around her to be "very religious," called me to "get the scoop" on Aimee.

Obviously thinking me *extremely* dim-witted (I don't know *how* she might have gotten that impression), she began to question me, "So...I heard Aimee and Hamid are divorced." "Is that true?"

Hearing my answer in the affirmative, she continued, "Whose idea was it, hers or his?"

"It was a mutual decision." I answered, "In fact, I believe it was quite friendly and civilized." "I can only hope I would behave similarly if I were in the same situation."

"Uh huh..." she replied, "So...Is she still a Muslim or what?"

At this question I bristled. She had reached the end of my patience with her obvious assumption that, because Aimee was a convert and not reared as a Muslim (as she was), she would discard her religion and relationship to God at the end of her marriage, as if her faith and conviction were never real, but only a role played for the benefit of her husband (a very common assumption, I am afraid).

I replied, "I don't know what you mean by that question. *Of course* she is still a Muslim. Why would that change simply because she is divorced? Why aren't you asking if her ex-husband is still a Muslim? Nationality does not dictate faith and commitment."

At this I received nervous laughter, "That's true." she said, and ended the conversation.

I didn't know if she really got my point, or if she simply realized she wasn't going to get the juicy scoop she had been hoping for, and backed off. What I did know was that I was glad that I wasn't at the place I was a few years ago when I would have run straight to my friend Aimee, told her what she had asked about her (less to help her, but more to share my frustration), and in turn, spark a retaliatory gossip session of our own. Instead, I was able for the first time to step back, shake my head, and react with amusement and acceptance rather than impotent rage against this woman and her prejudiced assumptions.

I'm not saying that, in my wisdom, I decided to turn a kindly heart to the woman out of a benevolent acceptance of the kind of bigotry her statement represented to me (If I had been wise, I would have refused to engage in the conversation at all). No, I wasn't thinking, "Oh well, nobody's perfect...Be easy on her." It wasn't about *her* at all. It was about my refusal to let another person shake me again. For this reason, I also decided to spare my friend the even more magnified pain that would result from me passing on the story to her. In short, I finally realized the simple truth that I had the power not to participate in the negative cycle of gossip, and in so doing, stopped it. Not out of a sense of superiority, but out of a sense of self-preservation and in acknowledgement of the hard-earned lessons I had finally gotten through my head—no benefit could possibly ever come from sharing gossip with another.

I decided once and for all that I would, in advance, consciously strive to not be so effected by backbiting (or other negative behavior) coming from other Muslims around me. This involved some concrete "realization steps" I thought about during the course of my daily walking and writing.

I determined that the first and most important thing for me to do was to accept once and for all that Muslims do horrible things. While it is true that a "horrible Muslim" is an oxymoron in consideration of the meaning of the term, I decided, for the sake of my sanity, to embrace the reality of the group of humans that make up the Islamic world, *as we experience them.*

For some reason, it was extremely hard for me to learn that Muslims were human like everyone else, and individuals at different stages of learning the many lessons of life. Some are good students and some are horrible students, and, like in academics, some never will learn. That fact is between them and God.

I decided to think of it this way—if a student studies Geometry, and fails to learn its principles, he or she will fail the class. Of course that is bad for them. However, their failure to learn the critical principles of Geometry does not affect Geometry itself. It, and its principles, remain the same whether the student misapplies its theorems or not. Simplistic, maybe, but the same goes for Islam.

Embracing this truth meant no longer suffering from the "but...but...that's not how it's supposed to be!" cycle that held me in its grip for so many years. Freedom from its grasp meant no longer having my faith and morale shaken every time someone acted wrongly.

Although a person may misapply or ignore the principles of Islam, and may even affect the lives of others though doing so, doing everything from backbiting and gossip on one extreme, to actual crimes and atrocities on the other, they cannot affect the integrity of Islam.

In celebration of my new acceptance of this fact, and in confirmation of my conviction never to have to return to my "but...but..." thinking, I decided to symbolically throw away my previous connections between the acts of the Muslim individual (the student) and Islam (the discipline). I vowed to myself never to submit to the shock, sense of injustice, and frustration that a melding of the two involves.

I loaded up my kids in their *Radio Flier* wagons, and walked to a small pond on the edge of our neighborhood. There, I picked up a rock from the shoreline, named it "My Belief in the Perfection of Muslims," and threw it into the pond. It was gone. My kids thought it was neat, and demanded a rather prolonged volley, to which I gladly indulged. Sure, it was a little silly. But it was fun, it was therapeutic, and, heck, it kept the kids happy. What more could you ask for?

The next time a fellow Muslim did something patently "un-Islamic," I would not have to feel that same sense of pain and frustration yet again. I had thrown away my mind's connection between the acts of individuals and their impact on my faith.

To this day, whenever I am tempted to return to my old thinking, I bring to mind my little rock resting at the bottom of that pond, and I imagine taking that rock and smashing the living daylights out of....wait...no, that's not it. No, I think of the serenity of knowing I discarded that old thought process, and I can move on positively.

The second step I took in releasing the hold negative talk had over my life was acknowledging the power behind inaction when it comes to gossip.

Before, I felt almost a compulsive need to share every negative statement I encountered in the course of interaction with others, a.k.a. "Can you believe she said that?!" I finally realized that there was power in deciding not to do so. I saw that, when I did share, it was usually serving only to vent frustration. Sure, it might be under the guise of seeking advice or guidance, but, usually, the motives were clearly on the whining side. The bad thing about this is that often, like sharing the latest horror story from the evening news over dinner, it does little to alleviate anything, and only serves to bring the unfortunate recipient of the talc down into the doldrums with you.

More than simply another tired rendition of "if you don't have anything nice to say..."—the power of not repeating the negativity of others (creating it ourselves is another matter) is a conscious decision to stop it in its tracks—after you there will be no avenue for it to continue. The more odious the comment, the more satisfaction it brings to know it is you that will squash it like a bug.

Like gossip and backbiting that originates with us, if we use will-power alone to resist passing it on to others, we are dooming ourselves to miserable failure. Backbiting is a sin, after all, and sins, by their definition are, above all, tempting. Like our motivations for backbiting, the urge to "pass it on" may spring from boredom, frustration, or jealousy. By looking inward and working toward what is missing in our lives that makes negativity in all its forms so attractive to us in the first place, we can find the power to lead a life of genuine happiness and fulfillment that no fleeting thrill could ever rival.

Looking inward has another surprising benefit when we are unfortunate enough to be the targets of malicious talk. In fact, this benefit has proved to be life-changing for me. I discovered this after I attended a *halaqa* for the first time run by a woman I had never met before.

I spoke to several women who attended a few of her previous lessons, and were very impressed, so, I decided I would dust off the old peds and go for myself.

I remember the topic of the night was *Behavior in the Mosque*, how to greet each other, pray together, etc. I found myself quite interested in the topic and impressed by the knowledge and manner of the speaker. I recall, she even answered a question that I had wondered about for some time, namely, what do you do when a woman next to you in a prayer line keeps drifting away? (Her answer was that you reach out and pull her back).

At the close of the meeting, the group broke up into conversation, and I talked with some friends, "See you next week...Blah Blah...This is a good *halaqa*...speaker really good...blah blah...nice dress, etc." I left the meeting fully intending to come again, full of good will and optimism.

Later that week, I paid a visit to a woman who had also been at the *halaqa* who decided to pass on to me, "You know Khadija (not her real name), the leader of the *halaqa* last Friday?" "She seems to think not very highly of you."

"Huh?", I asked, incredulous, "What do you mean?"

"Well", she replied, "I was talking to her after the meeting, and she said to me, 'You see that girl over there?' 'She's always a trouble maker.'"

Hearing this I was shocked, first, because I had never met this woman before, so how she could have branded me a "trouble maker" I couldn't fathom (otherwise, maybe...). Second, I could not understand how a woman could lead a *halaqa* on proper mosque behavior, end it, and immediately proceed to backbite.

In addition to the disbelief and sense of betrayal I felt at the fact that a "religious person" had behaved in such an un-Islamic manner (I had yet to conceive of stone throwing), I also felt personally horrible. Not only did this woman, for some unknown reason not like me, but she also thought, and was telling others, that I was a trouble maker.

At a point in my life when I was desperately interested in being liked and accepted, I felt like an instant failure. "Obviously, there is something wrong with me," my inner voice said. The fact that this woman had never met me before held no sway in convincing me to disregard her unfounded opinions. In fact, it actually made me feel worse that she didn't know me. My logic simply reasoned that someone else had told her I was a terrible person, and that meant (horror of horrors) that someone else probably didn't like me as well!

I never returned to that *halaqa*, and for many months I carried the wound and insecurity that I internalized as a result of her comment.

It wasn't until more than a year later, after I had begun examining my own reasons for being so attracted to backbiting, that I began to re-examine my feelings about that incident.

Upon reflection, I realized most others probably have the same, or at least similar reasons, for backbiting as I, with jealousy and insecurity at the top of the list. When I applied this reasoning to the *halaqa* leader, the possibility of her comment being, in actuality, more about *her* than about me, finally dawned. After all, if she was able to finish a lesson and backbite before even exiting the mosque, she most probably had some serious conflicting issues within herself.

Smiling, I realized how wrong and unnecessary it was for me to internalize and suffer over anything she had said. If I could look at all backbiting as a result of personal inadequacies within each individual (including myself) that are yet to be worked through, I never again would have to take to my heart another person's gossip about me. This is not to say that it wouldn't continue to make me at least momentarily angry or irritated with a person having something unkind to say about me (or anyone else I care about), only that I would not let what they say go to my heart and make it my reality.

This was a surprising, albeit, simple realization that couldn't occur to me until I looked at myself first, a realization that would prove to be an invaluable tool for understanding the motivations of those around me—even when I find myself the target of rancor.

Now, when someone says something nasty about me, far from internalizing what it is they said, my mind usually reflects on them, wondering what negativity must be going on in their lives—and what it is about me that resonates enough with them to warrant their attention. This has completely changed the dynamic of backbiting for me. It is no longer the words but the real motivations that stand out. Those motivations almost always go back to the self, not the target.

Strangely enough, this realization also opened up the door to the possibility of compassion and empathy for those who compulsively backbite. Not only is this good for handling those relationships which, although scarred by the hurtful words of one party, are not possible to sever, due to inevitable circumstances of life (family relationships, work and community ties, for example). Having empathy for the person that aims hurtful words is a release from having to carry bitterness. It's quite liberating.

I remember my husband mentioned to me the *hadith* concerning the goodness of a man who does not sleep with any hatred in his heart. At the time he shared this with me, I was at a point in life, when I admit, it actually made me angry. I was frustrated with the reality of Muslim life, and the way I felt there was such a huge gap between the Islamic ideal and actual behavior. I saw the lesson espoused in the *hadith* as yet another unattainable ideal, one based on forcing oneself to forgive all the horrible things suffered in a simpering attempt at perfection. This was not reality. How could you not have hatred in your heart?

Now, years later, I do believe it is possible to at least begin to come close to the ideal exemplified in the *hadith*. Like everything else though, I don't believe it is through willing to forgive, or even willing to be free of hatred. I believe it is only though an acceptance of the rather strange idea that nothing is really personal when someone acts out against us. We simply represent some lesson—something yet to be worked through for that person that causes them to lash out against what we represent that poses a threat to them, a weakness they have yet to conquer.

Unfortunately, accepting this idea as true doesn't mean complete freedom from anger. We are, after all, human. However, I do believe that realizing this can point to the path where holding onto hatred is no longer necessary, simply because we understand the real process.

I will be the first to admit that there are still times when what others have to say affects how I feel about myself. The fact is, I have noticed that there are certain times when another's judgment about me personally just seems to hold more credence in my heart of hearts and more sway over my mood, gray or sunny. In the warmth of praise, or in the midst of the coldest blast of criticism, my own struggle with self-worth rises up like the proverbial phoenix to remind me of its ugly and ever-persistent presence, a struggle that has helped to put many miles on my trusty Keds.

Unfortunately, a skewed belief in the importance of outside appraisals of our own worth is the number one impediment to the ability to live a life even marginally idyllic. If what other people think matters so much that each overheard complement or criticism is replayed again and again, heralding euphoric highs and devastating lows, all indicators point to a diseased perspective, and a perspective ill-equipped to see people and events for what they really are. A healthy perspective is the quality that determines either a life authentically lived and learned from, or a life lived for the approval of others. When we fail to see that that approval (or lack of it), is coming from some poor shmuck with their own lessons to learn just like us, we get off the track so much that it is all but impossible to learn anything meaningful, let alone live an ideal life as exemplified in *hadith*.

A sense of worth contingent on outside opinion is an extremely easy trap to fall into. Fortunately, it is also surprisingly easy to crawl out of. Even more surprising is how pleasant the trip out is.

Why not begin?

*Modesty is beneficial for maintaining
a certain moral fibre in various
cultures and should therefore be maintained
— but on the basis of faith:
not economics, politics,
or other forms of access and coercion.*
– Amina Wadud-Muhsin

*To be absolutely certain about something,
one must know everything, or nothing about it.*
– Olin Miller

Chapter Nine

Hijab

You're cringing, aren't you.

Not *hijab*...Not another word about *hijab*.

If you are like me, you are about as fed up with all of the rhetoric about the subject, for and against, as you can be.

If it seems like the predominance of focus in modern Islamic discourse has shifted from God and faith to *hijab* and the sexuality of women (which after all is what *hijab* is all about), you would be correct in your assessment.

From Saudi Arabia to Palestine, to Islamic communities in South Africa, England, and the United States, the Muslim world has become obsessed. You can see it everywhere in the literature, lecture circuit, and Islamic media. "*Hijab! Hijab! Hijab!* The cure for all ills! Wear it and you will be free from the tyranny of the fashion world, freed from the evils of sexual exploitation, protected from the possibility of rape and victimization."

Yeah, and if you believe *all that* I have a beautiful bridge that's currently available for purchase.

Not to be outdone, the anti-*hijab* camp is equally adroit in its propaganda. "*Hijab* is the symbol of oppression for Muslim women." "It isn't necessary, and only the uneducated and uncouth wear it."

Back and forth, back and forth, the never ending discussion goes, and we, like the audience of a particularly intense tennis match, look on in rapturous attention. Our collective interest is insatiable. Divided between those who wear and promote the wearing of *hijab*, and those who are, either steadfastly against the practice, or simply have chosen to abandon it for various reasons, we intently watch for which position will prevail;

one side hoping to find support, solace, and validation for the often difficult path that *hijab* demands (at least for the women that wear it), and the other seeking reassurance that their denial of the practice will not send them to the fiery pits of hell (as the pro-*hijab* camp asserts it definitely will).

At first, I found all of this discussion quite interesting. New to my community, and new to the experience of wearing *hijab*, all of this focus was right up my alley. Far from feeling that anything was amiss, my ears would perk up every time the topic was broached.

I lived *hijab*. I taught myself to sew, learned to thread my ancient sewing machine without a manual (what the heck is a bobbin?!), and spent hours hunched over it, turning out hideous *jilbab's*, scarves, and skirts (I cringe when I think of some of the outlandish getups I wore).

Not alone in my quest for the perfect Islamic image, I would impatiently wait for Fridays, when I could traipse off to the mosque, demurely shuffle past the men's section (sometimes covering my face, lest I appear wanton and tempt with my breathless beauty), and stride in, ready to take my place in the parade of Islamic fashion that was the Friday *halaqa*.

Now, one rule of life that I am still trying to beat into my head is the tendency of anything done on a superficial level to cause immense grief later.

We all know how it is when you clean the bedroom by throwing all of the clothes in the closet, pushing them in with your foot, closing the door and carefully poking in any stray items with busy little fingers. The room looks darn good to guests, but you know there will come a day when you will have to sort, fold, and hang all of those clothes. It will take a whole day, most of the clothes will have to be washed (there might be a *spider* in there by now!), and you will be so crabby by the end of it, your family will be like lambs to the slaughter when they dare to venture near.

So, too, was my treatment of *hijab* destined to be.

True, it felt great to experience of belonging *hijab* afforded. It was like having a backstage pass into a world where I still didn't really feel I belonged.

Let's face it. Our Muslim communities aren't the friendliest or the most hospitable of places. In fact, to many so-called "new-Muslims," the mosque can actually be a quite foreign and terrifying place. There, we often learn the hard way that the possibility of a quite embarrassing faux pas is but a step away. In such an atmosphere, at least looking the part is tremendously reassuring, both in providing a feeling of solidarity and belonging with the world of Islam at large (after all, most of us have at least on some levels had to walk away from the societies we have known) and in acting as a shield from the well meaning, but often insensitive "advice" from other Muslims.

The problem with this is, like the closet door, many of us are using *hijab* to cover up the reality of what is inside of us, in order to fit in, look good, and be acceptable.

Martha Stewart, a person I hopelessly desire to emulate in her achievement of peerless domestic bliss and tranquility, says, "Always use the correct tool for the job." This means you don't use a match to rid your legs of unsightly hair (My mother tried this clever trick, and can testify to its undesirable result). Similarly, you don't use *hijab* for anything other than what it was intended to be. Anything else might work out just great in the short term, but in the end is, like unorthodox hair removal, playing with fire.

On some levels I knew my motivations were hopelessly muddled when it came to just why I was wearing my scarf. For instance, I would completely dread the question, "So…why do you dress like that?" Each time it would take me by surprise, and, struggling with the swirl of trite explanations spinning in my head, I would grasp for one at random, rattle it off, and count myself lucky if what I said had some semblance of sense and conviction.

Looking back, I can definitely say that I was wearing *hijab* for three reasons. In order of importance they were, belonging, a wish to portray myself as morally superior, and a vague fear that God would punish me if I didn't.

I say looking *back* because at the time I couldn't admit, even to myself, that those were my motivations. To admit that would mean that everything wasn't right in my hastily constructed life as a Muslim. It would mean that I still had some things to figure out for myself, and if I didn't have it all figured out, all of those "know-it-all native-Muslims" would be right about me being a "clueless convert." They may even doubt my faith and sincerity as a Muslim. If I admitted, I reasoned, that I had some serious rumblings of revolt against most of the "rationalizations" for *hijab*—rationalizations that they seem to eat up like manna from heaven, while I focus on keeping my eyes from rolling like an out of control slot machine, wouldn't it mean their faith was stronger? Wouldn't it mean that I was just another "American troublemaker" that asks one question too many?

No way, not me. Let the other suckers face the derision of the Muslim community. I was going to keep all of my misgivings to myself, and then keep them so deeply buried that even I could ignore their doubtful chirpings. After all, I did have some great incentive for keeping properly complacent. My ego and sense of security in the Arab family I had married into were high up on the list.

My husband is from a very traditional family, from a tiny West Bank village in Palestine, a region where being considered a "strong woman" with firm, vocal opinions is far from desirable.

Being no dummy, I realized the odds of my being accepted in that society were quite slim indeed, especially if I couldn't play the game better than the home team. I had to be more Palestinian than the Palestinians, and since I had an insatiable love of Palestine since childhood, this was hardly a difficult stretch.

I saw the way others before me had been chewed up and spit out by Arab culture, and was determined not only to survive in it but to thrive—and, like the bridge that made my crossing into the Islamic community at home, I decided that *hijab* would also be my ticket to acceptance in Palestine.

My first trip to the West Bank was both one of the best, and one of the worst experiences of my life. There, I experienced the glory of Jerusalem, from the golden Dome of the Rock, to the ancient vaulted pathways illuminated by beams of streaming, smoke dusted sunlight, and filled with the wonderful smells of coffee, cardamom, and spices. I walked through the mountain fortress of Herod and stood on the edges of the immense, wondrous, and vaguely creepy Solomon's Pools, as the sun set and the wind whispered through the trees.

I also watched a man beat his wife until she lay whimpering under a truck in the peaceful town of Bethlehem, learned to become accustomed to having automatic rifles pointed at me and my loved ones, and had my rear-end grabbed so many times by depraved city-dwellers in Amman (which they were surprisingly adept at locating beneath my voluminous black *jilbab*), that it almost ceased to startle me.

In Palestine, I learned the practical rewards of wearing *hijab*. There, too, like my experience back home, *hijab* smoothed the way for acceptance into my husband's family.

People would come to see me for themselves ("Gotta get a look at the foreigner Hamad married..."), and exclaim, "Oh...she's just like one of us!", while my husband and family looked on with smiles of pleasure, and, maybe even a flash of relief.

I also noticed the quite different reception of a young British woman who happened to be there the same time as I.

Anne was a tall, thin, brunette with short, boyish hair.

When I met her, she strode into the room wearing Levi's and a t-shirt, appearing about as out of place as Marilyn Manson amid the Vienna Boys Choir.

Surrounded by aging ladies in traditional embroidered thobes and tattooed faces, and men clad in dishdashas and white aghals, valiantly but unsuccessfully attempting to keep their eyes securely in their sockets, Anne exuded a confidence and apparent ease that belied my understanding, and attracted my bitter scorn.

As my mother-in-law rose to greet her warmly, kissing her on each cheek and inviting her to sit down with us on the cushions lining the edges of the room, I was filled with nothing short of jealousy and a lurking sense of unfairness.

Here, I had worked so hard to cultivate an appearance and manner as close to Palestinian as a young blond woman from Oregon could get, suppressed all but a mere shadow of my real self, and worked for months trying to improve my meager Arabic, and this woman traipses in with her tight jeans and short sleeves, and fits in as easy as you please! It's just not fair, I fumed to myself.

I admit this line of thinking was a bit juvenile and petty...well, maybe more than just *a bit*. Nonetheless, such was my thinking as I sat in unspoken fury.

I began to make small talk with the object of my derision. Smiling the deceptively warm smile that I was so good at during that time in my life, I asked her how she was liking Palestine.

"Oh, I just love it!", she sunnily replied. "The people have been so friendly." "I was worried about how it would be, but now I think I am looking forward to my husband building a holiday house here."

"That's nice," I replied politely, and turned to chat with my sister-in-law until they rose to leave.

Although I now cringe at my attitude and behavior, looking back I understand that I was driven to such a negative reaction not out of righteous indignation, as I believed at the time (How dare she dress and behave so freely among these good, Muslim people...Has she no shame?!), but out of a deep insecurity within myself that poor Anne was unfortunate enough to evoke.

The depth of my insecurity was only underscored by my reaction to the news that she was, in fact, not as highly regarded or accepted by her husband's family as they led her to believe.

One of the highlights of my stay in Palestine was the traditional wedding party my husband's family threw for us.

During the festivities, I sat upon the raised platform that was my throne (actually a plastic chair covered by a rug) in my shiny white splendor (Ok, maybe my makeup would put any Sunset Strip street-walker to shame, but my hair was darn wonderful).

It so happened that Anne's mother-in-law and her friend were sitting directly in front of my perch. Making the mistake that many have made before and after them, they confused my inability to formulate an articulate Arabic sentence with an equal lack of comprehension. Thus, they prattled on without a care, as if I were about as much concern as a cat in the corner (a tendency people often have, and one I thoroughly enjoy).

"Why don't you have a wedding like this for your son and Anne?", the woman in front of me, resplendent in a shining pink gown, asked Anne's Mother-in-law.

"What for?", she replied. "He's going to divorce her anyway. He doesn't love her."

Oddly shocked, after all, I had also been deceptively friendly with Anne, I was filled with a mixture of disgust with the plumpish and somewhat dour woman before me, and her ability to deceive Anne about her and her son's true feelings toward her, and an overwhelming feeling of what can only be described as *satisfaction*.

My world once again made sense. Fitting in was rewarded, and, as the Japanese saying goes, "The nail that sticks out is hammered down."

Although I did have a small part of myself that was able to feel a measure of anger toward Anne's hypocritical in-laws, the shred of inner integrity that struggled to stay within me during that dark period of my life was easily overcome by my desire to find vindication of the life I had chosen.

I had the universal hallmark of the superficial and insecure, namely, the belief that anything or anyone in opposition to my chosen belief was a threat to me.

I basked even more in the warm glow of acceptance when the young nephew of Anne's husband said, within my earshot, "Lynn is worth a hundred Anne's because she wears *hijab*."

The pleasure I felt at that comment was immense. What other proof did I need to know that I was doing the right thing? After all, I saw Arabs, as the official judges of everything Islamic. If I were acceptable to them, well, what more could I ask?

After my return to the United States, however, a mixture of a few years of real life experience, and the combined effect of every book I could read on Arab culture and Islam began to turn a light on in my head (however dim), that perhaps Arab culture had more of an influence on the practice and perception of Islam and what was Islamic than Islam had on Arab culture.

I learned about things like the infamous "honor killings," where a sister or daughter is put to death by her own family members, usually a brother, father, or uncle, if she has been found "guilty" of adultery or fornication—even though in most cases the only "evidence" is a lack of blood on first intercourse.

Not only does this blatantly fly in the face of Islamic justice and jurisprudence, because of the lack of the required four witnesses, but also in the punishment inflicted—death.

Upon my second trip to the West Bank, I saw with new eyes how real an occurrence this is.

Flipping through the family photo album, I came across a picture of a pretty young girl. My husband's sister pointed to her and said, "She's dead. Her brother killed her."

It seemed her new husband wasn't convinced of her virginity on their wedding night, so, the next day returned her to her family, where the reports say, she was either strangled, or told to drink insecticide. She was quickly buried in secret and "honor" was restored.

This story had a profound impact on my heretofore, firm conviction in the supreme authority of Arab culture and the Middle East on Islamic life. What should have been obvious to me before, namely that Arab Muslims are human like everyone else on this earth, and as such, are just as given to less than holy motivations, came as a dawning realization.

I was left in a state of bitter disillusionment, followed by a period of intense distrust and often marked derision toward my self-appointed living examples of everything Islamic. With a sweeping blow, I had knocked them off of their lofty pedestal in my mind.

I embarked on my new quest to identify all of the countless ways modern Arabs behaved wrongly in the name of Islam.

From honor killings to wife beating, from the propensity of Arab culture at large to view women as mindless sexual and reproductive objects, and their maddening tendency to accept even the most blatantly ignorant man's "sage wisdom" as the infallible "Word of God" because he is included in the (rather loosely defined) category of the scholar (never mind that he may advocate female circumcision as a useful method of suppressing boundless lust in hot climes). I felt, that the vast majority of Arabs seemed to completely abdicate their own personal responsibility to reason. I was convinced that Alexander Pope's seventeenth century observation that, "Some people will never learn anything…because they understood everything too soon," fit the average Arab Muslim to perfection.

During this time, a friend remarked to me, after a particularly venomous tirade against the varied transgressions of the Arab world in general, as well as the particular cultural pressures I felt I was under as the wife a Palestinian, "Lynn, you seem so unhappy."

Surprised at her observation, after all, I never considered myself particularly unhappy, she said, "Well, it's just that you seem so *bitter*."

There are some things that people say that stay with you for life. For me, my friend's observation was one of them. What she said seemed so right, and so to the heart of the problem that I didn't have the ability to name for myself that I had no choice but to realize she was correct.

Thinking about it, I realized I had reacted with such bitterness because I had given the Muslim Arab in general, and my husband's family in specific, supreme authority in my mind over Islam and how

I could be a good Muslim. Basing my behavior, beliefs, and identity as a Muslim on what would garner their good favor and what would most closely emulate them, I had, of my own accord, placed in them a sacred trust.

When I realized this trust was (as it, in fact, *must* have been) misplaced, I was extremely angry and bitter toward them and myself. I wanted them to be what they weren't, and every time they showed that they were not capable of fulfilling the ridiculous role I had cast them in, I was filled anew with a fresh feeling of betrayal.

With the help of my friend I realized the never ending cycle in which I was mired. It was time to "get over it already," but I couldn't do that until I admitted to myself that, although my belief was intact, I had wandered down the wrong road with regard to motivation and practice. Nowhere was this more true than in my attitude toward my decision and motivation regarding *hijab*.

It wasn't going to cut it anymore to wear *hijab* because of its ability to garner support and praise from the Arab Muslims of my family and acquaintance. I no longer had trust that their motivations were always as lofty as I had once believed. Although many of them would beg to differ, I accepted for myself, once and for all, that they were no different from the non-Arab Muslim, and at times even *more* inclined than not to act out of motivations patently un-Islamic.

Although I wish I could say I learned my lesson both in not using any aspect of my practice, especially *hijab*, as a bargaining chip for acceptance, or by entrusting a belief that any person or group of people consistently behaves properly, or necessarily is in possession of the knowledge of the entirety of what constitutes Islamic propriety—lets just say I wasn't quite ready.

Instead of returning to myself, my relationship to God and the Qur'an, I turned to the community of what I called "thoughtful Muslims," or Muslims that demonstrated an ability to use their minds in an active pursuit of Islamic knowledge.

Wishing to get as far away from what I saw as the blind, and often disinterested acceptance of tradition and interpretation of many of my Arab brothers and sisters, I wholeheartedly embraced the world of contemporary discourse represented by the materials and discussions that predominated the English speaking Muslim world.

Hijab

I sought the company of "thoughtful" converts, as well as "educated" and introspective expatriate Muslims. The friendship I chose and the materials I read were still on the conservative religious side, but also were able and willing to bring up topics and discuss them in a way that interested me.

Never to be heard using the oft-used phrase of our "mindless" (we whispered) counterparts from the Arab world, who were painfully wont to say, "Its bad to ask too many questions," every topic was open for discussion, and no topic was more hashed and re-hashed than *hijab*.

We were staunch supporters of *hijab* all. We cried, "We are smart, we are powerful, the women in *hijab* can do anything!" And why not? I had seen enough suppression and sexism.

I fell right into the "Islam with style" that my "thinking" Muslims represented. No longer stifled by a contrived prudishness and culturally based sense of propriety, I could be seen swimming (in an Islamically acceptable swimming suit of my own design), roller-skating, and jet-skiing with bravado.

I felt that I had been reintroduced to a life of vibrancy—a life that I had become accustomed to living without as an "Arab wannabe."

I failed to realize that I had swung from one extreme to the other. It didn't feel like I had because I hadn't done anything "drastic" like become secular, remove my *hijab*, or stop praying. Instead, I had undergone a more subtle transformation of crossing from the extreme of mindless emulation of Arab culture (believing it was synonymous with Islam), to a reliance on a culture of excessive reason, a culture of people that could put the American Puritan movement to shame with their musings on the number of angels that could possibly be squeezed onto the head of a pin.

We considered such topics as, "Is it possible for God to create another God?" and, "Can God throw me out of his kingdom although he is everywhere?" to the more base, yet obviously interesting (based on the frequency of discussion) question of whether *Jinn* watch us in the shower, and if the prohibition of images in *hadith* extends to photo albums.

The polar opposite of Arab culture, we believed that there simply was a explanation to every possible question posed—simply reached through the faculties of reason.

Boy, this was right up my alley. I fairly pounced on every written word produced on Islam written from this point of view, from prayer to *hadith*, to women's rights. However, by far the most copious amount of ink seemed to have been devoted to the subject of *hijab*.

Pleased to no end by the possibility of finding a clear and usable answer to vindicate my position as a "muhajaba" (after all, my previous motivations had failed me miserably), I exhausted every book on the subject and moved onto the internet in my quest for more. I was not to be disappointed and soon found myself perusing through the world of the even more prolific web author.

Vindication was what I sought, vindication was what I found. It seemed, on the web, *hijab* was the solution for all social ills.

The following is just a partial list of all of the five hundred and one rational benefits attributed to *hijab*:

1. Protection from rape
2. Freedom from fashion's tyranny
3. Protection from skin cancer
4. Feminine appearance
5. Opportunity for *dawa*
6. Freedom from proposals for dates, etc.
7. Saves money (on clothing, hair spray, etc.)
8. Protects men from the wiles of feminine beauty
9. Allows other Muslims to identify you
10. Indicates piety
11. Protects from vain or frivolous thoughts about appearance
12. Eliminates competition (beauty, class, monetary), between women
13. Encourages proper Islamic behavior and propriety

With all of these lofty and wondrous reasons for wearing *hijab*, their combined force had a strange effect, an effect I thought to be unique to me, and perhaps a reflection of a lack of strong faith or my general tendency to pessimism.

Instead of feeling inspired, convinced and vindicated, I felt the more I read the more annoyed and skeptical I became. I was feeling a bit like a customer enduring the rhetoric of a "hard sell," and I began to wonder if anyone was really inwardly convinced that *hijab* was good and worthwhile because of the existence of these "reasons." Worse, I noticed that when I would try to use one of them in my continuing search for the "perfect" answer to the "why do you..." question, I would feel hollow and unsatisfied, almost as if I had just told a lie.

It was during this time that I began to write a book about *hijab*. Although I was inexplicably uncomfortable with the popular explanations for the practice, my intention was to use them anyway. Thus began my first chapter, a glorious exposition on the benefits of *hijab* and how wonderfully it has affected my life.

I wrote about fifteen pages in this vein, and then stopped. Exhausted, bored with myself and my train of thought (If you can call it thought), I decided to re-read what I had written. Trite, boring, and self-righteous were the words that instantly sprang to mind. Blocked, unsure of where to go with it or any other way to proceed, I didn't pick up the pen again for two years.

Then, I came across a book by Julia Cameron, entitled, *The Right to Write*.

In her book, she includes a chapter about honesty. Although just skimming through the chapter, my eyes alighted on a particular passage that shed an unexpected illumination on why the practical benefits and explanations of *hijab* had an unexplainable dissonance for me. A wall previously too high to see over suddenly came tumbling down.

Julia wrote,

> Writing is about honesty. It is almost impossible to be honest and boring at the same time...Whenever I am stuck on a piece of writing, I ask myself, 'Am I failing to tell the truth? Is there something I am not saying, something I am afraid to say?'. When the answer is yes, the writing shows it. There is a softness, a tentativeness, a rot to it that telling the truth instantly dispels.

Dusting off my old notebook and rereading my feeble attempt at my first chapter on *hijab*, I instantly realized the problem. I was a liar. I didn't believe one drop of what I had written.

"*Hijab* gives me a kind of respect I wouldn't otherwise have without it. It forces people to take me seriously, and gives me a confidence that I know I am not being evaluated on the basis of my sex..."—on and on I went, ad nauseum, enumerating the vast benefits I supposedly experienced on a daily basis since donning my scarf. I left such a dizzyingly profuse array of sunny truisms that the only thing I accomplished was a collection of paragraphs that would only have been convincing were they included in the dictionary's definition of *drivel*.

I imagined the image I might have evoked in a reader –glassy eyed, zealous, and able to rattle off complete absurdities with boundless conviction—I might as well shave my head and bring out a tambourine.

In my quest for rationalization, I had joined the ranks of those who were standing in a "deluge of words," only opening an umbrella to ward off the single, solitary, "drop of sense" that could be found to justify the practice of *hijab*—God.

I became sure of one thing. All the reason focused on *hijab* and applied in an earnest effort to quiet the revolt of the heart, all the energy expended in frenzied attempts to explain the doubts away and pound it into acceptance, and all of the attempts to convince, both ourselves, and others, of its righteousness based on supposed secondary benefits—in the end only served to create a hollow uncertainty in the heart and mind.

If we tried to explain that we should be Muslim, or that we are Muslim because Islam allows such and such a benefit, we would lose the essence of what it is to be one. So, too, does it zap the credibility of the requirement of *hijab* to attempt to make it falsely fairseeming to those who resist it, as if God couldn't have pointed out its many convincing benefits had he wished to make it more palatable to his servants. As Alexander Pope so eloquently expressed in his famous satire, *The Dunciad, book VI,*

> *For thee we dim the eyes and stuff the head*
> *With all such reading as was never read:*
> *For thee explain a thing till all men doubt it,*
> *And write about it...and about it:*
> *So spins the silk worm small its slender store,*
> *And labors till it clouds itself all o'er.*

It was strange, but it was a huge relief when I realized I no longer had to consider, remember, believe, or otherwise deal with any of the "rational" explanations of *hijab*. In fact, it all became very simple. I resolved that I would only consider the three verses of the Qur'an that deal with the subject. That's it. Either I believe that the meaning of the verses indicate I should wear *hijab* or not.

The three verses follow:

> *And say to the believing women*
> *That they should lower*
> *Their gaze and guard*
> *Their modesty; that they*
> *Should not display their*
> *Beauty and ornaments except*
> *What (must ordinarily) appear*
> *Thereof; that they should*
> *Draw their veils over*
> *Their bosoms and not display*
> *Their beauty except*
> *To their husbands, their fathers,*
> *Their husbands' fathers, their sons,*
> *Their husbands' sons,*
> *Their brothers or their brothers' sons,*
> *Or their sisters' sons,*
> *Or their women, or the slaves*
> *Whom their right hands*
> *Possess, or male servants*
> *Free of physical needs,*
> *Or small children who*
> *Have no sense of the shame*
> *Of sex...(24: 31).*

2.
> *O Prophet! Tell*
> *Thy wives and daughters,*
> *And the believing women,*
> *That they should cast*
> *Their outer garments over*
> *Their persons (when abroad):*
> *That is most convenient,*
> *That they should be known*
> *(As such) and not molested.*
> *And God is Oft-Forgiving,*
> *Most Merciful* (33: 59).

3.
Such elderly women as are
Past the prospect of marriage,
There is no blame on them
If they lay aside
Their (outer) garments, provided
They make not a wanton display
Of their beauty: but
It is best for them
To be modest: and God
Is One Who sees and knows
All things (24: 60).

[Please note I did not include the verses dealing with the wives of the Prophet (May God's Peace and Blessings be upon him), because I am quite certain that none of us qualify under that heading].

Of course, it is another question entirely whether these verses reflect the meaning we attach to *hijab*, and, although I have my own feelings on the issue, I will not expound on them here. I will say that I do continue to wear *hijab*. Yet, I will not attempt to persuade with my oh-so-lofty conclusions, for decision and conviction on this issue, must be left to the individual, and to the hearts conviction. However, I will deign to supply a few suggestions that have been helpful to me.

If you are one of the many for whom this "question of *hijab*" has been a matter that raises its head again and again, it is helpful to take some private time to think about it, when you can consider your *true* motivations for wearing it, or, as the case may be, the real inner motivations for not.

Stand back from the issue and get a new perspective on its relative importance. Realize the reality of the lack of proportion that has overtaken the interest of the community at large. After all, there are complex cultural forces behind the modern "*hijab* fetish" that have nothing to do with God or the Qur'an. To remember that there is nothing that we are required to consider aside from the words of God is sometimes surprisingly difficult. Putting this idea in mental focus can take a tremendous weight off the issue.

Hijab, like everything else, requires a conviction that is your own whether you wear it or not. However, I suggest that there is a difference between real and firm conviction, a conviction that comes from clear motivation and understanding, and conviction based on someone else's beliefs and opinions. Sooner or later anything done for the pleasure, good favor, and esteem of others (and this includes both wearing and *not* wearing *hijab*) will not be enough to support the hollowness that eventually becomes painfully evident—and not wearing *hijab* out of an inner motivation to be attractive or accepted (my two greatest temptations) is just as dangerous to the development of true integrity and faith as wearing it for acceptance and approval.

It is helpful to remember that the only function *hijab* must serve are these:

1. Modesty, as in verse 24: 31.
2. Identification as a Muslim, as in verse 33: 59,
to help ward off sexual advances.

To complicate, or allow anyone else to complicate the issue is to be dishonest. Worse, putting too much emphasis and importance on *hijab* ultimately sabotages true faith by sapping a great deal of mental and emotional faculties on something that is actually quite mundane. Further, trying to complicate, reason, or explain a thing too much has its own downfall, as John Wilmot wrote in 1684:

Whilst the misguided follower climbs with pain
Mountains of whimseys,
Heaped in his own brain;
Stumbling from thought to thought
Falls headlong into doubt's boundless sea...

The world is full of those who would have us do as they do, falsely pretending to be following the path of right while in actuality using persuasion of others as a balm on their own unaddressed doubts of motivation.

On this subject, Wilmot again has the perfect words. He writes;

All this indignation have I hurled
On the pretending part of the proud world
Who swollen with selfish vanity
Devise false freedoms, holy cheats and formal lies
Over their fellow slaves to tyrannize.

The only defense against this "tyranny," both in becoming its victim, or perpetrator (I have been both), is to spend time alone in introspection, reading the Qur'an, and practicing honesty within.

George Savill wisely wrote, "...True virtue hath ever been thought...to have its dwelling in the middle between the two extremes; that even God almighty himself is divided between his two great attributes, his mercy and his justice."

Extreme attention, emphasis, and debate on the subject of *hijab* not only becomes ridiculous, but damaging as well. It should neither be raised to an issue of excessive import, nor lowered to insignificance, for the potential for deceit lies on both ends of the spectrum. It is far better to allow the issue of women's *attire* to inhabit the position for which it was intended—the middle ground.

> Then which of the favors
> of your Lord will ye deny?
>
> – Qur'an (55: 13)

> Those who would storm the heavenly heights
> by fierceness and ascetic practices deceive themselves badly.
> Such people carry grim hearts within themselves;
> they lack true humility, which alone leads the soul to God.
>
> – Mechtild of Magdegurg

Chapter Ten
The Ascetic Life

Ah, yes, the lure of the ascetic life. Strangely tempting, considering how biased most of us are in our taste for the comforts of this world.

When I picture an ascetic life, I imagine in my mind's eye a scrawny old man with hairy legs, clad only in a loin cloth. He makes his way up a thorny, barren, and rock strewn path in a hot desert. His only possession is a knarled walking stick, and he tirelessly trods upward with the infinite "click, shuffle-shuffle" of his stick and worn sandals. Living only on the meager alms of other, less spiritual souls, he relentlessly plods on, squinting at the sun and gazing forward toward the mirage of enlightenment that awaits at the crest of his ascent.

Of course this man isn't a Muslim—for everyone says Islam is not a religion of ascetics.

So, maybe I should make my ascetic man a Buddhist or a Hindu, or even a Christian, in order that my musings be properly accurate. Yet, despite the fact that God, in his infinite wisdom, did not include asceticism as an aspect of the practice of Islam, despite the fact that it is actually discouraged, there remains an aspect of the Muslim soul that longs for it nonetheless.

Between the two extremes of the hedonistic and the ascetic life lies the heart of the average Muslim. Caught between the ever-so-attractive draw of the conveniences of this world, and the emotional, mental, and physical comfort and diversion they provide, and the consciousness of the transitory nature of those comforts, we are engaged in a tug of war between the two, everlasting.

In spite of the fact that the supposed virtues of the ascetic life are not a part of Islam, there remains a pull for many, a particular yearning of

The Ascetic Life

the soul that draws them toward the life of the ascetic. The same draw, I suspect, that moves people toward the monastic life in other faiths doesn't find an outlet in the life of the Muslim, and the effect in an individual who possesses this particular trait is often a tendency to compensate with a dogmatic harshness and rigidity of the kind we are all too aware.

In this mindset, a life lacking in color and beauty is often mistaken for virtue—all forms of celebration, all music, all of the wonderful scents of the earth are off limits for them, and, if they had their way, would be off limits for every other soul as well. For, bearing the universal mark of the insecure, they are incensed to the point of disgust when they recognize vibrancy and joy in another, and strive to eliminate all of the "wickedness" that a life including any buoyancy of spirit must, in their opinion, certainly contain.

Not to be confused with the truly pious, individuals of this bent try, often very successfully, to disguise themselves amongst their ranks, and, like so many things, cannot be distinguished by appearance alone, but by manner.

Unfortunately, many of those who are new to the Islamic community (and many who are not so new) find it difficult to recognize those individuals for what they are. Vulnerable, they open their trust and their hearts, unaware that they are admitting a skewed and diseased shadow of what Islam is into their lives.

Publius Syrus, observed, "The malevolent have secret teeth."

In our world, they are secret, and sharp.

What is so insidious about those who hide their malevolence behind a mask of religious piety is the devastating effect they can have on the faith of others.

From smug "scholars" who forbid everything from driving to freedom of divorce, from the mortal sin of the pink *hijab* to drinking sparkling apple juice (after all, it looks like champagne), and the wickedness of dancing at weddings (it's lewd, even if it is just women), the joys and pleasures are slowly leached out of life and slapped with the dreaded label of "*haraam*."

The following is a partial list of the things declared off limits by "knowledgeable" men and women:

- Music
- Perfume containing rubbing alcohol
- Dancing
- Swimming
- Makeup
- Henna
- Baby showers
- Wedding showers
- Bike riding (for women)
- Driving (for women)
- Rare steak (its bloody)
- Whistling (wanton)
- Fingernail polish
- Television
- Movies
- Singing
- Clapping
- Jeans
- Birth control
- Laughing aloud
- Speaking in the Mosque (women)
- Carnival rides
- Vacationing for pleasure
- Art (except calligraphy)
- Wind Chimes
- Non-Muslim friends
- Adoption
- Playing with dogs and puppies
- Parties
- English names
- Praying in English (even if it is the only language understood)

The problem with all of this is it becomes seemingly virtuous to invent or support prohibitions in Islam that are either based on opinion or out-and-out fiction, as if Islam were not challenging enough on its own well-grounded and unquestionable limitations.

It is nothing short of the same tendency toward asceticism that the loin-cloth clad man of my imagination would exemplify, the same self-created limits and constraints that have created a pleasure-free life of his own division, and the kind of life that makes others outside his sphere wonder in aghast awe why he would live such a life. It is also the same motivation that, after time, seems so saliently right, that the element of choice fades from consciousness, replaced by such a lack of perspective as to make suffering seem to be the only path to God. Not only is this wrong, but it is a lie of the soul, a false innovation that creeps onto our individual and community consciousness with a deadly stealth.

What is easily forgotten and so often overlooked in the current fire and brimstone atmosphere that is modern Islam, is that God in his mercy and generosity created beauty, joy and pleasure, just as surely as he created our ability to experience fear, pain, and suffering.

Samuel Johnson said, "Life is barren enough surely with all its trappings; let us therefore be cautious how we strip her."

We should be cautious, indeed, not only for our own sakes, but for the sake of others and the faith we risk destroying. In stealing the small mercies that make up the joys of life as given by God, and labeling them forbidden, we not only practice dishonesty, but the ultimate in ingratitude.

We can see the effects of this kind of thinking in the many ways we feel guilty for doing the innocent. One of my favorite examples of this is my "guilty pleasure" of taking off my scarf as I drive home on the country road that leads to my house at night.

Even in the dead of winter, I take off my scarf, roll down all the windows and blast the heat. I love the wonderful feeling of the wind whipping through my hair as I fly (careen my husband says) down the road.

The funny thing about this is, as I write I feel an air of scandal in my words, a certain trepidation that someone will fault me for my innocent indulgence, as if there is something shameful or wrong either in my action, or at least in my admission of it. This is my inner ascetic trying to take something innocent and make it wrong, and this is my fear, cringing in anticipatory expectation of others to do the same.

How many joys do we deny ourselves due to outside pressure or vague feelings of guilt based on foundations of speculation and fantastic leaps of reason? "Well X is wrong, so it naturally follows that Y is probably wrong as well."

If we become so accustomed to forbidding everything remotely pleasurable out of a misguided association of anything pleasant with sin, we eventually lose the capability to see the very real virtue that comes from the ability to accept the many different kinds of gifts God can bestow. For, I submit that the God-given lessons of joy are as beneficial to the health of faith as the lessons of pain.

I recently bought some Keds walking sneakers. White, leather, and platformed, they are the first pair of comfortable shoes I have had in over eight years. This because for those eight years I wore only skirts, blouses, and *jilbabs*—nothing that would look "right" with sneakers.

This year I finally bought my Keds, a pair of jeans, and a big Disneyland sweatshirt. I can't tell you the freedom and joy I feel from such a small act.

Previously, I bought into the notion (culturally based) that there was something inherently evil in jeans, and although, admittedly a size eight woman in a size six jean would certainly bend toward the immodest (no pun intended), a pair of comfortably sized jeans, a long shirt, and scarf qualify as modest attire in my book (as I am still trying to convince myself...Alas, it takes time).

I believe we must all ask ourselves, What joys have I denied myself? Under what pressures of the tyranny of the subconscious ascetic do I sway?

Whatever your false chains, I challenge you to throw them off— in the words of Isadora Duncan, "You were once wild here. Don't let them tame you!"

... God hath bestowed His gifts more freely on some of you
Than on others: to men is allotted what they earn,
And to women what they earn: but ask God of his bounty
For God hath full knowledge of all things.
— Qur'an (4: 32)

*Dans l'adversete de nos meilleurs amis,
nous trouvons toujours quelque chose,
qui ne nous deplait pas...*
— In the misfortune of our best friends,
we always find something that does not displease us.
— Francios duc de La Rochefoucauld

Chapter Eleven

Envy

Of all the varied human emotions, envy is by far one of the most utilized. It is also one of the emotions on which our feelings are most ambivalent.

On one hand, Muslims are among the most fearful of evoking envy of any people in the world. One has but to walk down any street in the Middle East to see this fact prominently displayed in the vast array of amulets, charms, and invocations designed to keep the "evil-eye" at bay. On the other hand, there is a shamefully strong temptation (of which we are hardly wont to admit) to shine in whatever manner we particularly excel, be it in beauty, knowledge, work, wealth, or even in suffering, in order to insure its evocation in the highest degree, even, or dare I say it, *especially* in those closest to us.

On one side, envy tells us when we see something in another person that we wish for ourselves. In this capacity envy can be a very useful tool of self-discovery. On the other side, envy can also become a self-destructive habit, eventually blinding us to every blessing in our own lives in favor of whatever we see as superior in the lives of others.

Jealousy is a shameful subject to discuss. Everyone feels it, everyone experiences it from others, but few people are apt to admit it. After all, admitting to jealousy is tantamount in our minds to an admission that another person is superior in some way to ourselves. That in itself is shameful. We also feel a tremendous guilt, especially as Muslims, about envy—that feeling it is tantamount to ungratefulness, a lack of depth, and a certain absence of magnanimity and goodwill that we will hide from others at all costs.

Like cholesterol, envy is made up of the good and the bad. The good comes when we recognize a trait in another that we wish to find in ourselves. We note it, usually in a friend, strive to emulate whatever it is, and eventually, if it is something we truly desire, make it ours.

Envy

For me, I felt this kind of envy regarding my friend Bushra.

Bushra is a fastidious housekeeper. At the time when I met her I was not.

It wasn't that I kept a dirty house, in fact, I felt I was always cleaning it. That was the problem. I was so disorganized, and had so much clutter and useless junk (that I worried I might need some day), that my home was in an almost constant state of disarray, despite my best efforts.

Enter Bushra. When I walked into her apartment, met by the smell of furniture polish and potpourri carpet freshener, pristine clutterless space, sparkling kitchen (where she kept layers of paper towels between each pot and pan), I was overcome with jealousy. I wanted that.

Honestly, it wasn't until I saw what Bushra had, and how she did it, that I realized exactly what I wanted—a pristine, clutter-free home (as clutter-free as you can get with small children anyway). Before, I knew I was frustrated with my home, but it was a vague, hopeless frustration. When I saw Busha's apartment, I finally had an image of the gap between what I had, and what I wanted. Miraculously, after several donations to *Goodwill* and a division of a solid weekly schedule of housework, I reached my goal.

The thing is, I never told Bushra she had affected me so much. I remember thinking that she might think me strange or shallow. But the fact was, she was the source of a very positive change for me, a change that, strangely enough, came through envy.

There is a different kind of envy, however, the kind of envy that is felt when you wish for something you see in another that is either impossible to obtain, like youth when you are old, long legs when you are petite, children when you are childless, the freedom of the childless when you *have* children, in short, anything that you cannot possibly have personal control over.

This kind of envy, when allowed dominance in a life, becomes a destructive force of bitterness, a drain of faith, and a source of hate. It is the kind of envy from which evil springs in the lives of the envious and the envied alike. Unlike constructive envy, nothing good can come from it. In fact, the more one indulges in it, the worse it becomes. Like the famous saltwater proverb, the more you drink from the well of envy, the greater the thirst grows for more.

Usually, when we find ourselves mired in the negative kind of envy, it can be distinguished from the constructive by one glaring symptom. It is painful. Whether I look at the beautiful, thin, fifteen-year-old and envy her youth and vitality of innocence that will never again be mine, or begrudge the success of a friend at some pursuit I have always dreamed of following but for some reason never have, the pain I feel at that moment is a siren blaring in my soul, telling me something is wrong.

When my friend, Natialie, was accepted to law school last year, I was wickedly jealous.

Going to law school had been one of my adolescent dreams. When I was thirteen I would sit in front of the television watching *LA Law*, and dream of the day when I, too, could wear beautiful and expensive "power-suits" and strut around a courtroom displaying my sharp as tacks intellect to its fullest glory and potential.

As life would have it (as it so often does), many factors of circumstance and personal choice teamed together to produce a different life. A life of writing, marriage, babies, and housework, and, although I could dress up in a suit (If I owned one), and parade back in forth in my living room expounding on literary theory, I doubt such an enterprise would be properly appreciated by my perplexed and agog family (one or more of whom would be frantically flipping though the Yellow Pages in search of "P" for "psychologist".)

Although I consider myself to be a happy and contented person in general, I felt a keen surge of resentment when my friend came to me with the wonderful news of her own intention to become an attorney.

As she described with a sigh the rigors of the study of law, her trips to the city to refresh her spirit, and her future plans for an international law career, my dirty diapers, soapy water, and battered notebooks became exponentially less attractive.

I sulked for two days, no longer finding my usual (I admit, somewhat strange) satisfaction in the gleaming shine of my kitchen table as I sat down to my morning writing session.

I knew that I no longer held any affinity for the study of law itself, but I still felt such a strong pang of jealousy, and, even worse, directed at a dear friend, that I was left in utter perplexity at the cause.

Eventually, I chalked it up to a reawakening of my old dreams that my friend had activated in her new pursuit. I moved on and thought no more about my ruffled feathers, until, during research on the topic of envy, I came across this, rather humorous, poem by Jonathan Swift:

> We all behold with envious eyes
> Our equal raised above our size.
> Who would not at a crowed show
> Stand high himself, keep others low?
> I love my friend as much as you,
> But why should he obstruct my view?
> Then let me have the higher post;
> Suppose it but an inch at most.

I realized I was no different from Jonathan Swift in my sentiments. I could have *written* that poem for goodness sake. It was clear to me that in my jealousy of Natalie, and in my jealousy in many other situations, I was reacting not to the thing itself, be it law school, beauty, whatever it was that sparked my envious side at the moment, but the recognition and approval that another's pursuit, attribute or achievement garnered for them. That was the object of my desire. I always wanted the "higher post," and, until I realized that as the real truth and motivation behind my jealousy, and understood not only why I so craved that recognition, but how to *get over it,* I would never be free from the painful and disruptive emotions that come from destructive envy.

Through experience, one of the things I have finally learned is that my own feelings can lie to me. Nowhere is this more true than with jealousy. As a result, I don't always trust this rather wily emotion, and now always try (as soon as I am able to regain my faculties of reason) to apply a very simple test:

1. Can I do anything about it?
2. Is this thing saliently important to me?

If the answer is yes to both questions, then I decide how best to pursue that thing, be it weight loss, learning a language, a cleaner house, kinder personality—whatever it was that sparked an envious admiration in the first place.

If, on the other hand, the answer is no to either one of the questions, I know that what I am feeling is destructive, and as such is coming from either insecurity or a lack of meaning in my own life that can only be remedied by an honest and vigorous soul search that has absolutely nothing to do with the object of my envy. As Joan Didion wrote, "To cure jealousy is to see it for what it is, a dissatisfaction with self."

To honestly acknowledge that dissatisfaction—and to strive to discover the ways in which to assuage it through change, is the only way to freedom from this kind of envy—and the only way to reach what we alone are truly meant to have, and to be.

> *If God had so willed, He could have made them a single people: but He admits whom He will to his mercy…*
> – Qur'an (42: 8)

> *Be not imitator; freshly act thy part; through this world be thou an independent ranger; better is the faith that springeth from thy heart than a better faith belonging to a stranger.*
> – Persian Proverb

Chapter Twelve

The American Harlot

There I sat in Salon Lorise in Bethlehem, watching in mute horror as the surly looking beautician's assistant applied yet another layer of makeup to my already clownish face.

It was the day of my "Palestinian wedding," and I sat dressed in a frilly white, gazing at my hair, coiffed to an incredible height in defiance of all of the laws of physics.

Harsh florescent lights hummed overhead, and I regarded my reflection in the large mirror before me. Blinking through mascara laden lashes at my transformed appearance, I couldn't help imagining that I would make an excellent cover-girl for *Raccoon Today*.

Working up the nerve, and desperately conducting an internal review of my meager repertoire of Arabic words, I managed to stammer out something to the effect of, "My eyes not pretty…Very much black, like smack. My eyes green, makeup not pretty to my eyes…"

At this my beautician stood back, regarded me quizzically, and, lips pursing in a smirk of derision, turned to the other assistant, working on the upturned face of my doe-eyed sister-in-law, and mumbled something unintelligible, but obviously disapproving.

Fearing I had just been woefully misunderstood, and worried my words had been construed as an attack on the abilities of my beautician to bring out the height of beauty in all she touched, I reluctantly dipped back into my shrinking vocabulary pool.

I pushed on, saying, "Just, I American." "Not face like Arabs…Too much black not good to my eye."

Exasperated, she deigned to reply, "*Khalas ya binit!*", "Enough girl!", and continued unabated.

Flushing with frustration and embarrassment, I turned beseechingly toward my sister-in-law for assistance, only to find her engaged in rapturous attention toward her own stunning appearance too profound to spare the attention necessary to apply to the correction of my plight.

I was faced with a decision. I could either relent and submit in acquiescence to my stylist's "vision" for my face, or I could, as communication had heretofore failed me, take matters into my own hands, procure the jar of cold cream that beckoned from its perch on the counter-top, and wordlessly remove the excess eye-liner and shadow.

Again, regarding my appearance in the mirror, I noticed a similarity between myself and Farrah Fawcet's character in *The Burning Bed*. Newly determined, my hand shot out to the jar on the counter, and without so much as a by-your-leave, (which I couldn't have expressed anyway), I began to remove the offending excess.

At this, my beautician as well as the assistant, a short woman with a bald spot the size of a silver dollar on the back of her head, and thick glasses that magnified her eyes into huge dark pools of black, stood back to regard me with undisguised contempt.

After a moment, my beautician again said, "*Khalis, ya binit*!" to which her companion sneered, "*Binit? Yimkin Binit,*" which translated to, "Girl? Maybe a girl", but meant, "She? A virgin, yeah, right!"

I understood what they said, and knew I had been insulted. I looked to my sister-in-law for support. Surely she would defend me.

However, apparently seeing nothing amiss in applying an insult so severe, an insult, if applied to *her* that would be on a level of murder-worthy, to *me*, she didn't raise an eyebrow, to say nothing of coming to my defense.

Although it was true that I had been married to my husband for two years prior to this "wedding," the beautician had no way of knowing that. Further, under any circumstances, the insult applied to anyone is rude in the extreme.

It was clear, however, that as an American woman, I was incapable of being insulted. Much in the same way a fish called slimy could hardly be offended, an American woman could not possibly be insulted by an insinuation, outright or subtle, that she is, shall we say, a somewhat loose character. It is simply a given.

My experience in Palestine is unfortunately not uncommon.

There is such a prevalent attitude in support of the belief in the inherent moral laxity of the non-Arab "convert" woman, in matters of behavior as well as understanding, as to be frustratingly epidemic. All that is necessary to appreciate how widely held and under what a breadth of acceptance this attitude reigns, is to sit at any gathering of American, European, or other "non-native" sisters. Without fail, each and every one will have a story. After all, misery loves company, and we all strangely delight in topping each other in our experience of this, rather frustrating, phenomenon. As Mrs. Oliphant said in *A House in Blumsbury,* "Even in misery we love to be foremost, to have the bitter in our cup acknowledged as more bitter than that of others."

My own friend Ann has a classic.

Walking in the mall one day, she spotted another Muslim woman walking in her direction. As is her correct habit, she stopped to say *salaamu alaikum.*

The woman, a middle-aged lady from Saudi Arabia, regarded my friend (who wears *hijab*), warily.

"Are you a Muslim?" the woman asked.

Wishing to be nice, Ann kindly refrained from pointing out that the answer was quite obvious, and simply replied in the affirmative.

"But you *are* an American." the woman observed.

"Yes." Ann replied, growing a bit miffed.

"How long have you been a Muslim?" she asked.

"Ten years...So, how long have you been in the U.S.?" Ann interjected, attempting to change the subject.

"Four years," she replied, making an impatient motion with her hand as if to brush away the question, and immediately continued, "But...Do you *pray?*" she asked, with a doubtful expression on her face, as if she had come across something that did not quite please her.

Now regretting having stopped to greet this woman, Ann countered, now offended, "Yes, I do." "Do *you?*"

The woman replied, "Of course! I am a *real* Muslim!" in haughty surprise.

As is often the case in these stories, Ann was overtaken by such a degree of astonishment, incredulity, and disbelief as to be rendered speechless.

The woman continued on her way, leaving Anne fuming in a wake of frustration and a thousand great responses that would have been lost on the woman anyway, had she had the presence of mind to offer them.

Both my experience in Palestine, and Ann's in the mall, reflect the same belief held by so many, namely that there is something patently inferior, unauthentic, and shady in our personalities, gleaned from our culture of birth that can never be fully erased by our acceptance of Islam.

We were, and we remain, tainted with an immorality, baseness, and lack of religious intelligence in the eyes of many "native-Muslims," despite our best efforts toward a life of faith.

Springing from the assumption that many of us are Muslim only because we happen to be married to a "native-Muslim," we are tolerated with a barely concealed derision by many sisters, and regarded as mere evidence of the sexual weakness of their men, overcome by the tempting wiles of the Western woman. As a result, we are tolerated by the community as a bit shameful, but Muslim nonetheless, although necessarily feeble-minded and in desperate need of basic and repeated instruction.

Thus, under constant scrutiny for our supposed, incalculable faults, we find ourselves subject to well meaning advice never ending, not to mention comments, assumptions and behaviors so insulting as to reduce the morale of anyone to shambles.

The ramifications of this attitude are far reaching, and can range from simple annoyance to out and out destruction.

Patricia, a kind, sensitive and sharply intelligent woman came to our city five years ago. She had just embraced Islam, broke off a relationship with her fiancée, and moved across the country to join in the local Islamic community, which she had become acquainted with over the internet.

The amount of faith, strength of spirit and courage required to make such a profound change in her life was truly staggering. It should have, in a perfect world, entitled her to a decent level of respect from her fellow Muslims, many of whom have never had to make a sacrifice for their faith bigger than finding a parking space more than a block away from *Eid* prayer. What she *got*, however, was quite different.

Married and divorced twice from "native" Muslim men who graced her with such abominable treatment as to prove intolerable, and faced again and again with insults, putt-offs, and exclusion from Muslim sisters, sisters who *should* have embraced her in friendship, Patricia was forced, for the sake of her own self-respect, as well as her sanity, to quit the community outright.

The tragedy of this experience was to be proven, not only by the cruel pain endured by this woman, who was a sister to us all, but in her ultimate decision to renounce Islam altogether.

Carly, another sister, also endured hardship on her road to Islam.

Coming from a devout Mormon family, Carly was subject to ostracism and the eventual loss of all contact with her family and loved ones as a result of her conversion.

Like the first converts in the early days of Islam, Carly persevered in her faith, feeling that, although the loss of her family was extremely painful, it was a price she was willing to pay for the sake of God.

Carly became an active member of the community, a loyal and supportive friend to many, and married a gentle and quiet Muslim from Syria. She moved in with her husband and his family in a shared home because her husband felt it was important to maintain as strong a connection with his family as possible.

For a while she was happy, enjoying life within a large family—a life she had missed in her time away from her own, and developed a particular closeness with her brother and sister-in-law while living there. Or so it seemed. For, that same family, the family that she worked so hard to please, helped to support, and truly loved, apparently saw nothing morally wrong with casting her aside as soon as her husband's citizenship became final.

These stories are sad, unjust in the extreme, and, unfortunately, hardly rare. Through incidents such as these, it is proven, again and again, that common attitudes toward "Western" and convert women are not favorable, a fact that most of us feel in our interactions with too many "native Muslims" on a regular basis. It is only more sad when one considers the chilly reception many receive from non-Muslim society as well.

We all know this is the reality we live with, and, although it is tempting in the extreme to rail against those Muslims who engage in such damaging and offensive words and behavior, I don't believe there is anything to be gained. In fact, it is naive, and frustrating to try to effect a change on the level of the perpetration of prejudice within Muslim circles, for it is a sphere in which we have absolutely no control.

People will think of us what they will. Ingrained attitudes are notoriously hard to change. The reaction, however, not the outward reaction to a particular event or comment, but the reaction *within*, the taking to heart of whatever it is, *is* with a surety wholly ours.

The most common and understandable reaction to the prejudice that many convert women experience is to place as much distance from any aspect of themselves that provokes this frustrating phenomenon as possible, an extremely tempting, yet also damaging, trap—a trap that entails a denial of the self of such a profound and basic nature as to be tantamount to a suicide of the soul.

I have often heard it said, when pridefully expounding on the diversity of the Islamic *Umma*, usually in the context of some *dawa* work, "The majority of the world's Muslims are not Arab," and "Arab and Muslim are not synonymous terms."

If this is the rhetoric espoused to the world at large, what is heard within the community is quite different, for here the maxim, "I can't hear what you are saying, your actions are speaking too loudly," heartily applies. The reality is that there is a perceived correlation between the terms "Arab" and "Muslim," whether we admit it or not.

Symptoms of this abound, from affected Arabic accents in native English speakers, to imitation of dress, manner, custom, food, and language, all in the misguided assumption, however subconscious, of the inherent superiority of all things Arab.

The practical rewards of this are many. For many non-Arab Muslims, the payoff of being "more Arab than the Arabs" ranges from heightened acceptance, assumption of piety, and increased freedom from annoying unsolicited advice and suggestion, as well as a large increase in perceived respect.

However, the other side of the coin isn't pretty—the drawbacks are severe yet deceptively and insidiously delayed.

In the early days of life in the "Muslim fold," once we pass out of the stage of naive idealism (a phase usually ended by repeated slaps in the face of this kind of prejudice), many learn rather quickly to conform to this standard. We reap the practical rewards conformity bestows, and fail to notice the price exacted on the psyche, until, often years later, the cost of the lack of authenticity that such conformity necessarily exacts, becomes abundantly clear.

If the fresh beginnings of our lives as Muslims provide an exuberance and excitement of spirit that allows a numbness toward the pain of the aspects of ourselves we blithely discard, the maturity that comes out of the passing of time (should God choose to grant it), wears away at that anesthetic effect.

Like a character in Ovid's Metamorphosis, "...delighting to wander in unknown lands and to see strange rivers, his eagerness making light of toil..." we traipse unfeeling through the annihilation of some of the very aspects of ourselves that conspired to lead us to Islam in the first place. Finally, hollow, depleted, and wondering what it is that could have lead us from such passionate hope and fulfillment in our early days, to the emptiness we feel at the apex of the elimination of our authentic lives, we realize with a shock the yawning emptiness that remains unfilled, despite our years of cramming in someone else's thoughts and ideals into the crannies of our existence.

The dawning truth is harshly difficult to bear, and is as stark and true as Rita Mae Brown's observation when she said, "I think the only reward for conformity is that everyone likes you except yourself." We suddenly realize that is not enough.

There comes a time in life, for some earlier than others, when the acceptance of others simply is no longer enough of a balm to ease the pain of the emptiness we have created. Finally, the consequence of all we have sacrificed comes to bear.

Matthew Arnold wrote in 1849, the poem *The Buried Life*. Although he was an English writer, hardly a Muslim, and his focus was finding meaning in a then, new industrial society, the poem speaks to self-created inauthenticity so eloquently, it must be included:

> Light flows our war of mocking words, and yet,
> Behold, with tears mine eyes are Wet!
> I feel a nameless sadness o'er me roll.
> Yes, yes we know that we can jest,
> We know that we can smile!
> But there is something in this breast,
> To which thy light words bring no rest
> And thy gay smiles no anodyne....
> But often, in the din of strife,
> There rises an unspeakable desire
> After the knowledge of our buried life;

A thirst to spend our own fire and restless force
In tracking our true, original course;
A longing to inquire
Into the mystery of this heart which beats
So wild so deep in us—to know
Whence our lives come and where they go.
And many a man in his own breast then delves,
But deep enough, alas! None ever mines.
And we have been on many thousand lives,
And we have shown, on each, spirit and power;
But hardly have we, for one little hour,
Been on our own line, have we been ourselves—
Hardly had skill to utter one of all
The nameless feelings that course through our breast,
But they course on forever unexpressed.
And long we try in vain to speak and act
Our hidden self, and what we say and do
Is eloquent, is well—but 'tis not true!
And then we will no more be racked
With inward striving, and demand
Of all the thousand nothings of the hour
Their stupefying power;
Ah yes, and they benumb us at our call!
Yet still, from time to time, vague and forlorn,
From the soul's subterranean depth upborne
As from an infinitely distant land,
Come airs, and floating echoes, and convey
A melancholy into all our day....
Only—but this is rare—
...The eye sinks inward, and the heart lies plain,
And what we mean, we say, and what we would, we know
A man becomes aware of his life's flow,
And hears its winding murmur, and he sees
The meadows where it glides, the sun, the breeze.

It is when we finally reach this point, "When the eye sinks inward, and the heart lies plain," that we realize that we actually *need* the thousand essences of life that make us who we are, that they are not as expendable as we once thought, nor are they candidates for exchange with those of another. We realize that the price of giving up our true selves is not worth the reward of outside approval that we reap in exchange.

Turning oneself into a façade of a person—affecting a love of beauty, interest, and behavior that does not come from the heart but from an imitation of the heart of another, is the death of authenticity. Not only must this eventually lead to extreme unhappiness, but also a struggle in faith, for how can you have a sense of relationship with God if the "self" is removed from the experience?

There are certain questions that must be asked in order to begin to break out of this situation, namely, why is the acceptance and approval of others so important in the first place? Has that desire abated enough to allow a rediscovery of authenticity? What are the parts of yourself that you remember and miss? How can one begin to excavate those traits that were buried long ago?

Time alone, writing, walking, and thinking, are excellent tools to help explore these questions. As John Ray said, "The wind in a man's face makes him wise," and Lord Acton, the English writer said, "Learn as much by writing as by reading." Their advice beckons to be seized.

Although we face certain frustration if we try to change the beliefs, perceptions and actions of others, one of the certain blessings of life is the power to change ourselves. Once the realization finally dawns that we don't have to care about misguided attitudes, the breath of freedom that comes in its wake is tremendous—but we first have to open the window to let that breath of air in. The best, and, I submit, *only* way to do that is to do as the Greek poet, Pindar, suggested, "Learn what you are, and be such."

If this is too vague, and you haven't a clue how to "learn what you are," consider, instead, the more specific words of Henry David Thoreau, "Pursue, keep up with, circle round and round your life, as a dog does his master's chaise. Do what you love. Know your own bone; gnaw at it, bury it, unearth it, and gnaw it still."—and be such!

And among His signs is the creation of the heavens and the earth, and the variations in your languages, and your colours: verily in that are signs for those who know.

– Qur'an (30: 22)

Behind every word flows energy.

– Sonia Choquette

Chapter Thirteen

Arabic

Language—it is the conduit of thought—the plumbing of the mind that carries the inner reflections of the individual into a form that can be shared with others, and a form in which the individual can gather the ideas and thoughts of human beings from a conversation at the dinner table to the written word, spanning the gap of centuries, oceans, and continents.

The gift of language is one of God's most miraculous. It is a gift that, arguably, makes us who we are. It is language allows us to "own" our thoughts—to translate them internally into a form that allows reflection, and reasoning. It solidifies emotion and feeling into the cement of words, and allows the formation of things as varied as opinion, belief, and thought to develop.

God used the medium of language to communicate his message to man in a form that was immediately understandable to him—and the fact that the words of God were delivered in the specific language of those prophets to whom the message was revealed, indicates the importance of personal fluency in the communication of *meaning* and truth.

It is highly doubtful that the message of Islam would have been as effective had it been revealed to the Prophet Muhammad (pbuh) in Hebrew. The Qur'an, itself, echoes this point, where it says, "*So have We made the (Qur'an) easy in thine own tongue...(19: 97).*"

In linguistics, the science of language, there is a fundamental principle which states that there is no idea that can be expressed in one language that cannot be equally expressed in any other. Notice, it is not to say that there is an equivalent *word* for every word between different languages, but that every meaning *can be expressed* through either a single, or combination of words.

Strangely, this is an idea bordering on the heretical in the Islamic community, where the Arabic language has been raised to a level of veneration of fanatical proportions, sometimes bordering on the ridiculous.

I recall one *halaqa* leader pontificating on the superiority of the Arabic language, declaring that English could in no way express the meaning of the original Arabic words, "*Allahu Akbar.*"

She reasoned, "You cannot translate *Allahu Akbar.*" "You see, it doesn't mean, 'God is Great', but, 'God is *Greater*', therefore, you *must* use the Arabic."

She went on to another subject, unaware that she had nicely and succinctly provided an excellent example of linguistic principle, as well as a superb illustration of a logical fallacy.

One of the surest and swiftest ways to a sound rebuke among Muslims of all backgrounds is to refer to a "translation" of the Qur'an. Eyes will snap and fingers will wag, "No, there is no such *thing* as a *translation* of the Qur'an. It *cannot be translated.*"

Many a new convert has been taken aback by this, often forceful response, not quite understanding the extreme error they have committed—and find themselves staring down at the "translation" in their hands, wondering what the heck these strange people are blustering about. Then, they learn the status of the Qur'an as a "protected" revelation, that is, the belief that the Qur'an is protected by God from any changes, any corruption, and that its words have never been changed. A five hundred year old Qur'an in Arabic is the same as one published today. Thus, a translation in whatever language, according to this belief, is not "The Qur'an," but, instead, a rough approximation of the meaning of its contents (with some translations being considerably more "rough" than others).

A useful analogy is reading the *Cliffs Notes* version of a work of *Shakespeare*. Although, it *is* possible to have a full and complete grasp of the meaning of a particular passage, the full feeling evoked by the beauty of the language is necessarily lost in the translation.

Consider this verse from *The Tempest,* one of the most famous:

Our revels now are ended. These our actors,
As I foretold you, were all spirits, and
Are melted into air, into thin air;
And, like the baseless fabric of this vision,

> The cloud-capp'd towers, the gorgeous palaces,
> The solemn temples, the great globe itself,
> Yea, all which it inherit, shall dissolve
> And, like this insubstantial pageant faded,
> Leave not a rack behind. We are such stuff
> As dreams are made on, and our little life
> Is rounded with a sleep.

Compare this with the meaning according to *Cliffs Notes*:

> Shakespeare here compares life to the stage, equating the fleeting quality of one to the other. He expresses his view that everything earthly will fade, including those Most revered, the palace and the temple. Each man's life is no more than a brief dream. Prospero says that the permanence of towers, palaces, and temples is nothing but an illusion; in reality these will ultimately dissolve and are not more real or permanent than the masque—or life—itself (58).

Clearly the meaning of the passage is fully explained, translated and understandable—minus the beauty and poetry of the original. Of course, although it is possible to read each of the *Cliffs Notes* to the works of Shakespeare and have a full grasp of the story and meaning of each, to do so would be pure folly.

What makes the works of Shakespeare great are not the stories themselves, or even the message behind those stories, after all, most of them are simply retellings of previous writings and tales. Instead, it is the poetry and beauty of the language that keeps it firmly entrenched in the cannon of English Literature, to both the delight, and horror of students, past and present.

When considering the Qur'an, however, the reverse is true. The meaning, the message of the book *is* of paramount and unquestionable importance. Yet, the language serves a function far more lofty than the mere beauty and evocation of emotion as seen in Shakespeare. For, in the case of the Qur'an, the original Arabic serves as both the gate-keeper of authenticity and textual integrity as well as an unparalleled and unique example of poetic beauty so miraculous as to be impossible to reproduce.

In this sense, I like to think of the original Arabic as a guard, posted over the words of God, serving a function that can never be filled by

English or any other language of translation. However, I submit that, according to linguistic principal, it *is*, at least in theory, possible to fully render *all* of the meaning fully and completely into any of the varied languages of the earth, provided the translator is honest, intelligent, and in possession of an *internal fluency* in *both* languages.

Whether such a translation currently exists, or even comes close, is up for debate, and is a subject on which I will not attempt to embark. Such an examination requires the same fluency and understanding as the production of the translation itself, in both languages in question. I'm afraid that, not only is such a qualification quite rare, it is certainly not one to be found in my person.

Let us suffice with the translations (and I use the common meaning of the English word without any of its political implications) and consider the question of those Muslims that, I suspect, make up the majority of the Islamic community worldwide, for whom Arabic is not only a foreign language, but also one that, in most cases, is not likely to be mastered on a level of internal fluency.

It is only logical that those Muslims, a group in which I am definitely a full and card-carrying member, are required to use a translation to gain access to the meaning of the Qur'an.

Unfortunately, God's use of Arabic as the source of his final revelation (ironically, in order that it may be *understood*), has today become a source of linguistic arrogance for some. Worse, the veneration logically heaped upon the Arabic of the Qur'an has somehow extended itself to Arabic *in general*—and it is in this atmosphere that an assumption somehow creeps into the collective Muslim consciousness that Arabic is the language of God—the only one that He understands, and the only one that He listens to.

Those holding this attitude possess the inexplicable belief that Arabic is a language is superior *in itself* to all other languages. This is in spite of the fact that most who hold this opinion are only truly fluent in Arabic, and, as such, are hardly qualified to make that assumption. The evidence of this belief is everywhere in Muslim life, but nowhere is it more apparent than in the attitudes surrounding prayer, *du'aa*, and social interaction.

In their heart of hearts, many non-Arabic speaking Muslims are ambivalent about prayer.

Again and again, we, as Muslims, are enjoined to be "fully present" at our prayers, to never allow them to disintegrate to the point of just "going through the motions" in a kind of glorified version of calisthenics.

It is strange, then, to consider the fact that "scholars" seem to unanimously agree that prayers *must* be performed in Arabic, even by those Muslims who have a very marginal (at best) understanding of the language.

It seems even more strange, when the majority of the world's Muslims fall into this category, to consider "mindless repetition" a defect in prayer when the very requirements for its performance, as agreed on by these scholars, create an ideal atmosphere for this dynamic. I often wonder if the fact that all of the scholars of Islam are necessarily fluent in Arabic has blinded them to this obvious truth, and that they have fallen prey to the tendency to forget that not everyone in the world is blessed with a similar understanding of the language. Like the old women in my husband's village, who could not comprehend that I did not understand their language, and sought to facilitate my comprehension by way of ever-increasing volume, I wonder if the scholarly conclusion regarding the question of Arabic prayer was not based on a similar unspoken (and perhaps, unrealized) belief in the ability of the world at large to somehow comprehend the Arabic words just as they do.

When considering this question, I prefer to believe the latter explanation—because I have found the "official" reasons for this requirement to be sadly lacking in sound reasoning.

It seems that the general consensus on the origins of the requirement for the use of Arabic in prayer seems to follow the following line of thought: Reciting the Qur'an should always be in Arabic because translations never capture the meaning of Arabic, and many of the subtle nuances are often lost in the translation. Further, saying the prayer in Arabic provides a sense of unity with the Muslim world at large.

One man explained it like this, "If you go to China and they are saying prayers in Chinese, unless you understand Chinese, you will not understand what is going on."

Another man wrote, "It provides unity on the *Hajj*."

What I find strange in these rationalizations is their utter lack of logic, the most glaring example of which exists in the first, namely, that a translation would lose some of the meaning of the original. This argument sets up the obvious question—*Are the words of prayer offered for the benefit of the supplicant, or for the benefit of God?*

Although the Qur'an often speaks of doing things, including prayer, "for the sake of God," it is clear that the meaning is not to be taken that God *needs* the good deed, the charity, or the prayer, but that "the sake of God" means, more accurately, seeking the good graces and approval of God. The deed or prayer is not done to help God in any way, but for the benefit of the soul. The prayer is done in a quest for the pleasure of God. This is evidenced by the verses, "*To God belong all things in heaven and earth; verily God is He (that is) free from all wants*...(31: 26)," and "*O ye men! It is ye that have need of God: but God is the one free of all wants, worthy of all praise* (35: 15)."

Prayer is also performed to maintain a close connection to the reality of God, and the real purpose of life. In this capacity, it results in a higher likelihood of upright behavior, as well as a method of revitalizing faith throughout the hectic days of life. When considering these two very important functions of prayer, namely seeking the pleasure and approval of God as an example of devotion and adoration, and its function as a touchstone to remind the supplicant of his or her purpose in this life, it is clear that the common rationalization for the performance of prayer is not a reasonable one.

To assert that prayer must be performed in Arabic to prevent the loss of meaning in this light is ridiculous. When one considers the *function* of prayer, meaning is of paramount importance *to the individual*. If meaning is important, it then follows that a significantly greater level of meaning is available in a language in which the individual holds an understanding.

It is true that a shade of meaning is lost. However, I submit that, even in the worst case (and I don't believe the translations currently in use are *that* bad), fifty percent were lost in translation, the remaining fifty percent is more than would be understood if Arabic, a language in which the individual holds no real level of comprehension, were used.

The second rationalization for Arabic prayer holds more weight logically.

It is quite convincing to assert that it is a good thing to have a universal language uniting the Islamic world, a language that allows for such diversity as required in *Hajj*, where it is possible, and, in fact, routine, for two people to stand side by side after being, just a few days before, on the opposite sides of the earth.

The fact that those two people can experience the unity and brotherhood (no sexism intended) of prayer, is directly due to the Arabic language. That cannot be denied.

After conceding, however, to the fact that the necessity of Arabic prayer is valid, especially in the congregational sense, there remains the question of the Arabization of Islam, and all of its practices, including those that are, for all intents and purposes, private. Whether that is useful, beneficial, and good, or whether it can actually be damaging is a question worth considering.

It cannot be argued that there are certain aspects of prayer that are exclusively private, or, at least lend themselves to privacy. These are aspects of prayer in which the full understanding of the supplicant is a necessary component. Including the portions of the daily prayers that *are not* Quranic verses, but instead are derived from *hadith* and tradition.

The daily prayers consist of one required verse, the *Fatiha*, and another optional one. These, it is argued must be performed in Arabic (although I, personally, say them in English after I say them in Arabic). As for the remainder of the prayer (with the exception of those portions said aloud in congregation), as far as I know, there is no convincing rationalization for the requirement that it be said in Arabic. To do so neither preserves authenticity, as they are not from the Qur'an, nor to preserve unity, as they are offered silently.

It is perplexing, then, to understand why non-Arabic speakers are repeatedly instructed to mindlessly memorize and recite these portions when there is no rational reason for the practice.

What possible good can come from the parroting of words that are not understood, and how can this practice be encouraged in light of the very real danger of drifting into mindless repetition?

Nowhere is this trend more of a travesty than in the performance of *du'aa*, the very essence of which is imbibed with the earnest supplication of the heart of the individual Muslim.

The *du'aa* comes in various forms and occasions, from the worry of a mother over the sickbed of her child, to the guilt ridden sinner seeking forgiveness and strength, to the more mundane angst-filled student, facing the first page of an important exam. The individual supplicant seeks the aid, closeness, and comfort of God with an urgency, hope, and belief that captures the very essence of true faith and trust.

To somehow muddle this relationship, to impose any artificiality or ritual, necessarily flies in the face of the function of *du'aa* itself. Yet, this is exactly what is being done when Arabic is made the language, de rigueur of *du'aa*, regardless of the supplicant's ability to understand it. To insist on that is akin to expecting the native Arabic speaker to use Latin, and is no less ridiculous.

Nowhere in the Qur'an, or *hadith*, does it expressly, or even indirectly, require the *du'aa* to be performed in Arabic. However, again and again, earnestness is expressed as essential.

Arabic is not a mystical language, nor was it chosen because it is the "language of God." However, the simple fact is, Arabic has taken on such a required role in the practice of Islam in a time when the majority of the world's population has no real understanding of the language that one wonders at the cause.

It cannot be denied that God is quite clear in his reason for choosing the Arabic language to reveal the message to Muhammad (Pbuh), "...so that it may be understood." Yet, somehow, in spite of the clear explanation, the unconscious belief has somehow been created so that the collective Muslim consciousness somehow imagines that Arabic is not only the only created language (the others mere "developments," and not God-created miracles in their own right), but also the only language God *understands*.

If this is not the case, I must admit that I am at a loss to explain the existence of the countless "how to" manuals for *du'aa*, as well as the detailed and painstaking transliteration of Arabic prayers suitable for occasions as varied as protection from the evil eye to requests for aid in times of personal grief—the premise of which is to help the non-Arabic speaker perform the *du'aa* properly (in a form that God will accept), in Arabic, who must struggle to read the transliterated words, mangled out of recognition both by transliteration and the accent of the poor finger-reading soul.

Now, at the risk of offending those pious Muslims, of whom I do not doubt their sincerity, faith and good *intent*, let me assert that there is nothing so unjust and damaging to the establishment and *maintenance* of faith than the placement of a wall of incomprehensible language between the words of the heart and God.

There is a famous Italian proverb that says, "A little truth helps the lie go down."

I will (begrudgingly) accept the authenticity argument for the necessity of prayer in Arabic for Quranic verses, and I am even more convinced when the point of unity in public prayer is introduced. However, I will not accept any such application in throwing a blanket of Arabic over *du'aa* as a liturgical language *in itself.*

I am absolutely tired of sitting, even in a congregational prayer, hands uplifted, piously (at least appearing so) beseeching God for requests I have absolutely no comprehension of, and struggling to follow the cadence of the emotional, often tear filled, voice of the Imam in hopes of inserting "*ameen*" at the appropriate point—all this while feeling an acute absence of the emotional connection so evident on the Muslims around me, blessed with a comprehension of the words.

If I am tired of that, I am through with struggling through a litany of Arabic in my own personal *du'aa*, as if the Arabic words were a kind of magical spell required to open the lines of communication between myself and God.

Once and for all with a radical-fist raised, and armed with the absolute, and what should be obvious, knowledge that *God understands all of the languages of the earth,* I stand in refusal of *the assertion* that I must say a *du'aa* in any language that I do not understand.

I raise the flag of English, my beautiful, God-given language, the language that brought the truth of Islam to my soul, and the language that carries my hopes, dreams, and prayers, and refuse to allow the idea of its illegitimacy to continue in my consciousness.

Perhaps you find me a bit extreme, standing at my kitchen table, fist raised in a stance that would make any seasoned Greenpeace activist wild with envy (wait, let me put my coffee cup down), but the strange thing, other than my appearance, is that holding the view that it is possible and good to pray in a language other than Arabic is a radical one, especially in the current Arabophile (coinage, mine) environment. In fact, I guarantee that such a stance will evoke some sort of disapproval in the majority of Arabic speaking Muslims (and also in a good portion of those who aspire to be). Of these Muslims, some genuinely consider it almost a sin to use any other language in a religious capacity, although I challenge them to come up with a convincing argument in support of their view.

Still others worry such a position will be the end of the incentive to learn Arabic. A third group believe that Arabic is a language so superior as to render prayer offered in any other tongue base and meaningless.

As for those who worry that a belief in the importance of the understanding that only a true fluency can provide will necessarily diminish the incentive and importance of learning Arabic, I believe this is unfounded.

The ability to read the Qur'an in the original Arabic, and to be privy to the vast information of generations of Muslim scholars is a testimony to the obvious importance of the Arabic language, as well as the immeasurable merit of its mastery. However, I do suspect that, save by the most gifted, or the very young, when achieved as a non-native language, Arabic will always take a back seat to the native language as the medium of thought and feeling—the sources from which private religious devotion and supplication naturally spring.

The evidence in support of this fact is legendary, for, caught in a moment of fear, pain or excitement, a multilingual person will most often revert to their native language and cry out in that tongue.

Ironically, it is also the very argument that Arabic speakers use against the "translation" of the Qur'an that supports the irreplaceable place of native language in religious feeling and expression.

An excellent example in support of this fact, is that an Arabic speaker will often read a "translation," compare it to the original text, and say "It just doesn't capture the *feeling*" of the Arabic, and will attempt to re-word the English to capture whatever it is they feel was lost.

Perhaps those who so intently assert the superiority of Arabic *in itself* lack the kind of perspective gained from putting themselves in the place of others, and consider themselves so special and superior as to be unable to consider any culture, language, and way of life in general, worthy of respect and esteem. After all, there is a fine line between pride in one's language, culture, and identity, and outright bias.

There can be no question about the existence of a very definite atmosphere against the use of English, or any other non-traditional "Islamic language" (Farsi, Urdu, Pashto, etc) so much so that new converts are astounded to learn that it was not necessary for them to change their names (often to non-religious Arabic ones) except in rare cases ("Christian," for example).

Further, many feel they are required to use Arabic expressions and terms, such as "*deen*," "*salat*," and "*alhamdullah*," when English would not only just as effectively suffice, but perhaps be more inclusive in certain settings—an English *halaqa*, for example.

Ultimately, this is harmful to faith, harmful to a sense of self-worth, and harmful to the propagation of Islam.

We so often say and hear that Islam is a religion for all mankind. An over zealous and unfounded insistence on its Arabization (in all areas), not only flies in direct opposition to that premise, but points to an underlying racism hiding under the guise of piety.

Ironically, the place to begin to change this problem, is not in the Arabic speakers of the Islamic world, but in the converts, and other non-Arabic speakers—individuals who not only suffer from this bias, but actively participate in its perpetration.

Many converts (myself included) are so excited to begin our lives as Muslims that we forget that it is all too possible to be a bit over-zealous in our "out with the old" mentality, and we throw the baby right out with the bathwater. It is only years later that we find ourselves realizing the importance of what we so thoughtlessly discarded, often in the midst of a crippling doubt and low self-esteem that is all but inevitable.

Personal change leads to public change. What we don't value and protect in ourselves will not be valued or respected by others. An engendering of respect only comes with self-respect and authenticity. Self-respect and authenticity can never come while one is actively accepting the idea that one is somehow "less-than."

It is a frustrating exercise in futility to imagine that we can change the attitude of those who find the use of other languages frightfully unorthodox, or those who find "converts" themselves in need of unending moral, educational, and behavioral instruction.

It is said that no one disrespects a person without their permission. Although there are definite exceptions to this statement (so much so that it can be quite maddening), there remains a grain of truth in it that cannot be denied.

To imagine that it is possible to engender respect in those who hold a firm belief in the yawning chasm that exists in the heart of the "convert," where, in them, resides the regal glory only a "traditional" background of birth and blood can bestow, is especially ridiculous when we, *ourselves*, are so convinced of its existence, that we stand at the entrance, handing out lanterns to illuminate the depths of depravity within.

When we believe we are lacking in respect to another person, due to any intrinsic part of what makes us who we are, or any quality we possess that is not related to faith, belief, or behavior, it is impossible to hope to engender respect in those who hold no belief in the possibility of its existence within us.

Instant respect cannot be created for the use of English, or any other "non-native" language, or for converts themselves through any means, be it educational campaigns, lectures, or outright nagging, without the necessary *internal* change first.

I will be the first to admit that, in my early years as a Muslim, I considered myself vastly inferior to native Muslims, and was actively engaged in a pointless struggle to emulate them to my fullest capacity.

Language and culture were my first targets of acquisition, although I admit, I was considerably more successful in cultural emulation than in mastery of Arabic (where I am still wont to say things like, "I going to store yesterday"), I strove to look, act, cook, clean, eat, sleep, and breathe as unlike the American woman I was, as I could get. Yet, I found doing so did not increase my faith, nor even maintain it.

Although I believe there is nothing wrong in striving to acquire aspects of a culture, society or language that one admires *through their merits,* there is a difference between that and trying to completely erase one's own cultural and linguistic identity in a belief *in the inherent superiority* of another.

Those of a traditional Islamic background are often the first to decry any identification with a particular culture or society, and as such, are hardly wont to acknowledge the damage such self-imposed emulation can produce. However, I suspect, upon careful observation, the oft-repeated maxim, "We are not Arab, Pakistani, etc...We are Muslim.", in most cases, begins to wear a bit thin.

Culture and language are God-given building blocks from which personality springs and is able to find expression, and as such, are indispensable aspects of life that are only departed from either in the solitude of retreat, or within the embrace of a tradition different from our own. As such, I suspect that, even proponents of the "We are Muslim" argument, adhere to their own culture with a unrecognized force as real as the beating of their hearts.

The truth is, the vast majority of those who deny the importance of culture and language, only deny culture and language different from their own. The proof of this assertion is, in most cases, born out in the daily life of those individuals, should they care to reflect on the matter—in everything from the music, and literature in their homes, to the food and drink in their kitchens.

Whether we care to admit it or not, our capacity to live an authentic and honest life is greatly diminished in direct proportion to the amount of effort we put into erasing our own cultural and linguistic identity without just cause.

We all talk about the importance of one *Umma*, and that culture, language, nationality, and the like, should not be a cause of undo pride. I believe this is absolutely right. However, it is not the same thing as believing it is necessary that we all be the same.

Cultural and linguistic anthropologists assert that culture and language are tools (I depart from standard anthropology and linguistics only in my addition of "God-given") that allow the individual to effectively process the information of the world around them. Culture and language allow for communication and ease of interaction with which we all live in the world.

It is possible to be one *Umma* while embracing our differences at the same time, *and* while acknowledging the merit and worth of those differences in as much as they do not conflict with the tenets of Islam.

It is worth noting that, whereas any talk about the acceptability of English (or any other language) or non-Arab culture is widely considered to be divisive, it is often perfectly acceptable to tout the superior merits of Arabic, and even Arab culture, despite its rather disturbing tendency to stand in direct opposition to many of the principals of Islam.

Here, as in many areas of life in Islamic society, a certain strength of character and willingness to admit accurate knowledge is essential, for the exclusionary atmosphere surrounding languages that do not originate in the "Islamic World" is of such a degree and prominence that it takes a strength born only of experience to develop the emotional self-respect and confidence necessary to withstand its pressures.

Samuel Butler said, "Words are the clothes that thoughts wear."

A silk, beaded *shalwar khameez* may be a beautiful and appropriate garment to wear on *Eid*, but I wouldn't choose it for a comfortable

Sunday afternoon at home.

Just as jeans and a good, baggy sweatshirt make up my wardrobe of choice when I am in my own element, most at ease, and in my private sphere, so will English ever remain the clothing of my thoughts in their most private capacity. It is only after many years of struggling against this notion that I have accepted it as natural and even good.

My language is a gift from God that I cannot, and finally, *will not* deny—thank God with a little time, and experience behind me, I no longer have the wish to.

*On no soul does God place a burden
greater than it can bear...*
– Qur'an (2: 286)

*...A grief without a pang, void, dark, and drear,
a stifled, drowsy, unimpassioned grief,
which finds no outlet, no relief
in word, or sigh, or tear—*
– Samuel Taylor Coleridge

Chapter Fourteen
When Things Are Bad

As I write, I am sitting in the back of my car with my fourteen month old daughter, Amani, watching her explore the wonders of my empty iced coffee cup and straw.

She finishes off the remaining drops of coffee with a relish that foretells her probable fate of becoming a seasoned coffee addict like her mother.

It is one of those moments when I am blessed with that feeling of joyful contentment that comes with the pleasure of the everyday. The day is slow, my mind is not in its usual state of harried confusion, and I am pleasantly surprised to find myself so simply happy.

I watch her play, still fascinated by the straw, now looking at me with her big, brown eyes and a smile of delight as the sun dances on her orange necklace of tiny plastic stars.

Thank you God, I say, actually using "*alhamdullah*," one of the few Arabic expressions that hold an instant meaning in my heart. Only…I can't help but feel a twinge of fear, knowing how fragile such a moment is in my life, and I suspect, everyone's.

Amani focuses on my pen and reaches across the page of my notebook, intent on laying possession to what I refer to as *my toy*.

I return to the page after she tires of my pen (I was forced to offer a cracker as ransom), and I focus on that feeling of fear that I usually am too afraid to mention.

I realize this fear is relatively new to me, and it is one that has developed, not due to experience alone, as I previously thought, but to a mixture of experience and the passage of that stage of youth where resiliency and natural hope hold court with a façade of such strength that their true fragility only becomes apparent well after the appearance of maturity.

Samuel Coleridge wrote in 1802 an amazingly poetic description of this youthful resiliency of joy in his Ode to *Dejection*,

> There was a time when, though my path was rough,
> This joy within me dallied with distress,
> And all my misfortunes were but as the stuff
> Whence fancy made me dreams of happiness:
> For hope grew around me, like the twining vine,
> And fruits, and foliage, not my own,
> Seemed mine.

Now, more and more, I notice the absence of the optimistic hope that was once mine as well, and I find that I experience each moment of joy with a twinge of fear. I no longer possess a moment of happiness as I once did—with a sense of entitlement and surety of the promise of more to come.

Instead, as in this moment, the smile on my lips is betrayed by a shadow of sadness—the very same look that I would occasionally glimpse on the face of my father as I was growing up.

Then, as a child, I was confused, even annoyed by the look of it. *Stop it,* I would think, *don't be so dramatic, so sappy, so depressing.*

I would hasten to make some witty, or alternately, biting remark to make his look, his sad smile, go away. It made me uncomfortable.

It seems that only the mixture of time and experience has the power to produce the alchemic transformation of the clear smile of youth into the smile I now fix on the joyful face of my daughter—a smile she is not old enough to notice, nor wax uncomfortable…In time.

I am not sure if those who are not parents feel the same emotion, or whether the mixture of time and experience must necessarily contain the particular component of a child—the delicious smell of babies fresh from naps, the puppy-dog scent of a little boy coming through the door after a day outside in the wind, or the hot little hands of a toddler, asleep with a fever, wonderful and awful at the same time. I am unsure, maybe because I became a parent at a relatively young age, and only noticed its emergence after the birth of my son, whether the ingredients necessary to produce this transformation must include the bond of parental love, rather like the addition of baking powder in a cake recipe.

Regardless of its origin, one of the striking things about this feeling, this happy sadness, is its ability to magnify even the most mundane into the treasured. The clear smile of my daughter would perhaps go unnoticed, the request from my son to "come hug" would go postponed while I diligently (manically) go about the all-important task of folding laundry...Even the sight of my husband stacking a load of firewood (a chore in which I do not partake, lest there be spiders in them, there, logs) would be free of my musings on the awful possibility of days upon days without him, should he leave this life before me.

Yes, clearly this feeling is a blessing, a gift of appreciation that allows me to recognize the individual moments of life as the precious gifts they are.

Yes...Yes...And if I had a choice it is also a feeling I would banish from my emotional repertoire faster than you can say "Prozac."

I hate it. In fact, I consider this feeling akin to my childhood relationship with Brussels sprouts. Knowing their supposed health benefits did not abate my horror when faced with a steaming plate of green, smelly goodness before me—just as knowing the appreciation and poignant beauty evoked by the painful knowledge of the transience of joyous moments does not abate my wish to be free of the knowledge once again.

Such is life. Brussels sprouts are harvested and bound for the plates of children everywhere, and souls continuously pass out of their cocoons of youthful exuberance into bewildered adults, suddenly in full possession of the sad smile.

Yes, it is good for me, but it's also still hard to take. Harder still are those actual moments of personal tragedy when they eventually do come—as they do for us all.

Then, we find ourselves sitting at a traffic light gazing at the people in the cars passing before us, in wonder that their "lives of details," shopping, cooking, arguing, laughing, continue while the world for us has been stopped in its tracks. The merciless inevitability of death, sickness, or tragedy drawn from the well of endless possibility comes crashing home.

It is a boundless shock, and once experienced it is never to be forgotten. Each moment of joy ever after (and amazingly enough, moments of joy do come again), is tainted by its memory. And it is the experience of everyone of us blessed with a life that stretches into adulthood.

Unfortunately, as Muslims, most of us live in communities that are, to put it kindly, not equipped to assist those suffering in a time of crisis.

Muslims are as human as the rest of the world, however, especially within societies in which Islam is not the dominant religion, our equal propensity with the rest of the world to succumb to difficulties is often ignored by our own communities. Muslims are faced with everything from divorce, death of a loved one, illness, economic emergency, or even crime, yet our communities are infamously ill-equipped to offer assistance or even simple solace.

The most glaring culprit contributing to this reality is the particular cultural and social dynamic characteristic of "ex-patriot" Islamic communities.

One incident in which this was definitely the case involved a young and beautiful woman in the midst of what was quite possibly the most tragic experience of her life.

Her husband lay dying in a coma, after being diagnosed with an advanced, and previously undetected, stomach cancer just days before, and several people from the local Islamic community were on hand to conduct a waiting room vigil in support of the young couple.

As commendable as the intention was, I was dismayed to see a discussion commence considering whether it was *halal* or *haram* to disconnect the life-support on which the young man had become completely and irreversibly dependent—a discussion not conducted in a loving or helpful way (the young wife had not asked for advice), but in the manner of a debate, as if there were not a very real and immediate emotional despair in their midst.

I have seen cases of domestic violence, divorce, and even rape, treated with everything from blatant culturally based sexism, hostility, indifference, to outright derision, when leaders or ordinary members of the Islamic community were turned to for aid—and time and time again, I have seen nothing short of gleeful interest on the faces enquiring of a community member in crisis, obviously hoping to replenish their store of relatable gossip (the worse the better).

The sad and honest truth is that many communities are sorely lacking in the resources, training, and compassion necessary to be a source of solace or guidance in a time of crisis. Even more sad is the fact that most Muslims come to realize this, rather unfortunate, fact during a time in their lives when they are at their most vulnerable.

Having been through one of these periods as I waited for test results on my son, results that would determine whether he had the devastating chromosomal abnormality, *Fragile X*, I must admit that the Islamic community, with its share of highly competitive and gossip-prone individuals, teamed with its track record (at least in my local area), of being less than supportive in times of crisis, was absolutely the last place I wanted to turn for emotional comfort or advice. In fact, strangely enough, it was the words of an anonymous nurse (almost certainly not a Muslim) that pointed me in the direction of the only comfort I was to find in those difficult weeks.

I was on the phone with the office of my son's neurologist, in an effort to get some clarification on the specific symptoms of the disorder. As I spoke to the nurse, I was distressed to find myself unable to stop the wave of sobs overtaking me.

Unable to ignore my obvious distress, the woman told me, "Go hug your children and hope for the best."

"Ok", I said.

"Are you really going to be Ok?" she asked.

"Well, I guess I don't have a choice", I replied.

"Yes, you always have a choice..." she said, 'You can get on your knees and pray."

Strangely enough, it was these simple words, spoken by a Christian, in all probability, that pointed me toward the only relief I was to find in those days—prayer.

It sounds hokey, it sounds trite, it even sounds vaguely sacrilegious to find comfort in the words of an unbeliever, after all, it expressly says in the Qur'an, "*Let not the Believers take for friends or helpers unbelievers rather than Believers...(3: 28).*" However, I also believe that inspiration and mercy from God can come in many forms.

One thing I learned from this experience is that, in times of despair, a thick fog of misery descends so quickly that the obvious is quickly obscured from view.

Although I had been praying during this time, my prayers had been mostly along the lines of, "Please make my children okay." It never occurred to me to pray for comfort in itself—to seek solace from God to simply ease the pain.

I did, I really prayed, and actually began to look forward to the coming of the next prayer time (something I had never done before), and, there with my children playing on the floor at my feet, I found a calm serenity and an unexplainable knowledge that everything would be Okay, no matter what.

It is no small thing that I could find comfort in prayer, when I was in such a state that no words, no conversation, no tears, no sleep—*nothing brought relief.* I was in one of those situations when nothing *could* offer relief, the kind of pain that brings an instant kinship of feeling to all those who ever contemplated suicide, a kind of pain like childbirth that one longs to escape at any cost. That prayer was able to bring relief from this kind of despair is no small testimony to the power and mercy of God.

Had I sought solace in any other avenue, I am sure I would not have made it through that time. Further, that those sources of comfort that usually serve me well in times of everyday difficulty held absolutely no power over actual despair proved to me that only God *is* sufficient—that the verse, "...*God is your best Protector and the best of Helpers* (3: 150)," was true. Perhaps everyday difficulties of life might lend themselves to helpful advice and aid from other, well-intentioned souls, but, in a time of real and extreme crisis, not only is it impossible to "pull yourself together," so, too, is it impossible for anyone else to truly help or give comfort. It is a time when there is absolutely no relief to be found in platitudes, advice, or moralizing, however well intentioned.

It is days since the writing of the first words of this chapter, and I now sit at my kitchen table, pen again traveling over the page. My baby, Amani is now attempting her first bumbling steps across the kitchen floor, barefoot and tenaciously holding onto the sparking pink toy car she uses as support. Her hair is in a ponytail at the top of her head. It looks decidedly like a palm tree.

I begrudgingly accept the fact that a morning such as this will not always be peaceful or happy. As surely as the sun rises and sets, so, too, bad times will come again. I only accept this because I must. To be honest, I am scaring myself just by writing this down, and find myself asking God to protect myself and the ones I love.

But I also know from experience that there is help and mercy from God even in the worst circumstances—a help that is not to be experienced from the words, actions or embraces of others.

Unfortunately, this subject is almost never discussed beyond the level of moralizing. In fact, the closest I have ever heard the subject come usually centers around the tendency to beg God for help in times of adversity, only to forget all about it once delivered from the icy grasp of despair, as in the verse, "*When trouble toucheth a man, he crieth unto Us...But when We have solved his trouble, he passeth on his way as if he had never cried to Us...(10: 12).*"

Although warnings against improper behavior always have merit (and ingratitude of such a degree as found in the Quranic verse is definitely an excellent example of how not to be), there is at times such an emphasis placed on warnings, injunctions, and recrimination, that the practical steps that *should* be done in a particular situation are all but obscured, leaving each individual Muslim to flounder in a darkness that could have been lit by the light of those who have traveled before.

Real anguish is a part of this life that we are all bound to experience. For me, the absolute only thing that got me through it in one piece is in private prayer between myself and God—in my own way with my own heart.

It seems obvious enough, but it took a stranger over the phone to remind me of it.

Sometimes it is easy to forget that we, as Muslims, have very real practical problems that require straight, direct, and private soul searching and prayer. Unfortunately, there isn't much emphasis placed on the importance of this information within Muslim circles.

Although going over the fine points of Islamic life has its place in community discourse, there comes a time when honest compassion, true understanding, and quiet guidance are called for, and discussions, judgment, and debate are best left behind.

I truly believe that if such qualities were found and practiced in greater quantity within our communities, it would serve the average soul in a far greater, and a more authentic capacity than what is currently available—for when periods of tragedy and suffering come, as they must come to us all, it would be nice to find a gentle hand from within the fold of Islam to guide the way. It is the least we can do for each other.

A Note on Depression

In Muslim circles, it is not popular to speak of depression. In fact, depending on which cultural factors are involved in any given situation, it can be downright taboo to even discuss the possibility that someone may be clinically depressed.

Often, either depression is thought of as something that is entirely under the control of the individual and, as such, can be "snapped out of," or at the other extreme, as a form of mental illness carrying a stigma of insanity.

Either way, the depressed individual is not likely to be motivated to seek outside assistance for what is, in reality, a real and treatable medical problem—and is even less likely to share their experience with other Muslims.

Depression is highly treatable in all of its forms. Counseling and medications such as Paxil, Prozac, and Buspar, or a combination of both, are highly effective in combating its symptoms.

The most common signs of depression are:

- Depressed (sad) mood.
- Change in sleep habits (sleeping too much, or difficulty sleeping).
- Loss of interest or pleasure in daily activities and activities previously enjoyed.
- Weight gain or loss.
- Loss of energy.
- Thoughts of death or suicide.

If these signs apply to you, I urge you to see your doctor and tell him/her about your symptoms. Not only is there nothing shameful about it, but it is simply an unnecessary illness that can be treated.

One would never think of living with an infection that could be simply and effectively treated with antibiotics. Depression should be no different.

...and He gave you hearing and sight and intelligence And affections: That ye may give thanks to God.

– Qur'an (16: 78)

Everything keeps its best nature only by being put to its best use.

– Phillips Brooks

Chapter Fifteen

Women's Work

One of my most beloved family traditions is the ritual of Saturday morning coffee with my husband.

I just love to wake up, brew an exquisite pot of Starbucks (after all, we *do* live in the coffee capital of the world), and settle down at our dining room table to discuss life. My husband acquiesces to this little demand on him because that's just what good husbands do. He thinks I don't know he secretly would rather start the day remote control in hand, but I recognize the signs—the shifty eyes, his neck straining to achieve maximum sound reception of a basketball game, mysteriously on in the next room.

I don't worry about it. I know that, sooner or later, my son will awaken and begin *his* Saturday morning ritual. The cartoons will come on. My husband's neck will relax, his eyes will clear, and he will say, "What honey?"

It was during one of these morning conversations that I was commenting on my inability to get any writing done during the previous weeks.

At my suggestion, we had embarked on the rather daunting task of completely remodeling our kitchen. The entire process was clearly and effortlessly accomplished in a single half-hour episode of a home-improvement program on the *Discovery Channel*. I was convinced we could do the same. After all, how hard could it be?

I convinced my husband, who was rather dubious about the idea, that we could accomplish the same glistening white-on-white masterpiece of American kitchendom, sans assistance.

Four weeks later, we sat enjoying our coffee, gazing at the results—not exactly as flawless as on television, but nice enough, and a substantial improvement on the previous seventies-era ambiance.

Women's Work

True, we had almost killed each other in the process (there is no surer test of the mettle of a marriage than a co-undertaking of home improvement), but we finally had a pretty kitchen, as well as the important fringe benefit of having depleted our monetary stores to such a degree as to make retaining respective divorce attorneys all but impossible for some time (time enough for the memories of mid-renovation hostility to fade).

So, there we sat, discussing our mutually shared excitement of getting on with the neglected business of our lives, when I mentioned how anxious I was to finally finish my book.

At this, my dear, usually wisely sensitive and socially astute husband, with a flourish and a snort declared, "Oh well...you have plenty of time...its not like its exactly *critical*."

I was stung.

Having my writing (picture me in a beret scribbling in a coffee house), my book that I had been steadfastly pouring my soul into for the last seven months *not critical*, dismissing it as if it were some cute hobby to be tolerated, perhaps amused by, but not taken seriously, was extremely hurtful.

Seeing my expression, and regaining his senses, my husband, in an effort to implement hasty damage control procedures, blurted, "What I meant was, there's no hurry...you can finish it anytime..."

I knew his intentions were good, but I wanted to end this conversation before it had an even greater impact on my morale—and, not wishing to open my heart's calling to further dismissal, however unwitting or unconscious, I quickly changed the subject.

This exchange got me thinking about the infamous, yet strangely passive resistance women meet from those closest to them, those whom they love most and are most loved by, when a decision is made to follow the "authentic calling" of the soul.

As anyone who has embarked on the pursuit of a personal love knows, the worst thing you can do is to allow a cloud of doubt to creep into the endeavor. Whether writing, following an entrepreneurial or professional calling, or doing anything that truly has the investment of authentic desire, there is an inherent fragility and need of protection that comes with the territory.

Lest I sound too "new age," let me explain what I mean by "authentic calling."

It is only in the "modern age" that we have departed from the idea that each individual is blessed with a specific gift that is truly and uniquely theirs. Today, it is almost foreign to embrace the notion that each person has a calling or vocation that is an integral part of their identity. Instead, we, especially as women, have been taught to believe "we can do anything" as well as anyone else. In my mind, the question is not whether we *can*, but whether we *should*, or even want to.

The great German writer, Johann Von Geothe, wrote, "Everyone undertakes what he sees another successful in, whether he has the aptitude for it or not." Unfortunately, unlike Goethe, the vast majority of people seem to embrace the tendency toward empty emulation as a virtue (as long as it might garner riches or approval). Sadly, Muslims are no exception.

Few stop to consider the possibility that, in following the shoulds, the esteemed professions, and the guaranteed money makers or money less, but people-pleasing endeavors, we are wasting God-given talent in the process.

I have often heard the concept of *risq*, discussed in *halaqa* lessons, where, usually, it is directly associated with money or material provisioning. It seems we almost never consider it on the level of blessings of ability or situation—the concept that each individual is imbibed with a particular gift or quality with which they were meant to excel, an existence that is uniquely suited for them, and a quality that, when utilized, fills the soul with joy and purpose.

I know women who not only excel, but find contentment in the complex arts of homemaking (with the proof found in the exquisitely organized linen closet—scented, organized sheets, towels, pillowcases, comforters bound in satin ribbon), the smell of baking apple pies, fresh bread, and home cooked meals, happy children and beaming husband.

There are other women for which this is a struggle. The linen closet is a closed door bursting with a jumble of towels, sheets, and who knows what (At least its clean!), the only thing that comes out of the oven once bore the name of *Swanson,* the children are in front of the *Nintendo,* and the husband is harping for the hundredth time about the lack of matching socks.

Instead of finding fault, used to preconceived notions of how a woman should be, perhaps it is possible to consider that one woman is ideally, authentically, and internally gifted with a calling to the domestic, and finds her sustenance (the essence of *risq*) both emotionally and financially through the nurturance of her home and family, and, through either luck or conscious choice, created a life around this ability.

The other woman, however, perhaps by ignoring her own inner voice, or in listening too intently to the voices of others, followed a path that was not hers, now finds herself hopelessly lost as a result, neither finding joy nor natural ability in the domestic realm.

Conversely, in the "working world," one can find women who excel and find genuine satisfaction in their careers and are horrified at the thought of giving them up—while there are others who work through either "necessity" or coercion, watch the clock, and dream of home.

A great deal of discontent and struggle comes from ignoring the internal signs that point toward the genuine—what is internally right.

Nathanial Emmons wrote, "One principal reason why men are so often useless is that they neglect their own profession or calling, and divide and shift their attention among a multitude of objects and pursuits."

My college experience was a monument to the truth of these words.

I changed my major five times from cultural anthropology to agricultural engineering, back to anthropology, to business, and finally to English.

The thing was, these changes were prompted, with the exception of English, by heeding the voices and opinions of others—parents, friends, and even my husband—not by inner prompting.

Anthropology was easy and good for a beginner, engineering was practical and prestigious, and business could prepare me for a "career." The only problem was Anthropology was too easy and felt pointless, engineering was completely beyond my grasp of mathematics, and business alternately bored me to tears, and terrorized me with required courses in accounting and statistics (out of which I earned a C- and a D respectively).

When I finally switched to English after the wake up call of a miserable term in business, and its accompanying C- grade point average, I surprised myself and those closest to me by going on to become, and remain, an honors student ever after.

It's not that I finally buckled down and began to study. In fact, I did study, but not half as hard as I did in my other majors. Instead, I found that for some reason I was just good at English, that I naturally liked literature and writing. This liking was not due to will alone, but to a natural inclination that was inside of me.

It is said that success and contentment come when love and will intersect toward a single focus. Could it be that love of something can point to the seat of *risq* within, while it is will that carries the strength, work and discipline that brings that love to fruition? That cooling culinary masterpiece of a perfectly risen soufflé, scientific discovery, exquisite embroidery, successful business, or heartbreaking Quranic recitation—could they not be the essence of God-given sustenance?

If so, how does one know when one is (or is not) living a life in full utilization of true purpose—the unique platform for doing good in this world?

Gary Zukav, the author of the best-selling book, *The Seat of the Soul*, summarizes an answer to this question eloquently;

> What does it feel like to remember your souls task?....When the deepest part of you becomes engaged in what you are doing, when your activities and actions become gratifying and purposeful, when what you do serves both yourself and others, when you do not tire within but seek the sweet satisfaction of your life and your work, you are doing what you are meant to be doing. The Personality that is engaged in the work of the soul is buoyant. It is not burdened with negativity. It does not fear. It experiences purposefulness and meaning. It delights in its work and in others. It is fulfilled and fulfilling.

In this light the harried housewife is viewed, not as lazy, incompetent or lacking, but as a woman who has forgotten or ignored the signs toward her individual, genuine God-given gifts.

As Muslims, many of us are not used to looking at ourselves, or others in this way. Instead, the reality of life for the majority of Muslims is that we (like it or not) live under the shadow of some of the most demanding cultural expectations of just what makes a woman great, desirable, and successful in the world, and almost none of them have a thing to do with authenticity, Islam, or what is "best" for anyone.

Keeping up with the Jones's not only has been elevated to a high art, especially between women, but all eyes, male and female, assess the worth of a woman by the degree in which she sacrifices herself to live up to those expectations.

Even more difficult, when convert women marry men from "traditional backgrounds" they often carry the burden of their own culturally created beliefs about what makes a "good woman" and add the cultural beliefs of her husband's background as well. Combined, these expectations can form a wall as daunting as a field of land mines between a life authentically lived and a life of halted dreams and wasted abilities.

Although much lip service is given to the topic of women's rights, the reality of many, if not most, is far from the rather progressive Islamic ideal.

Few women are strong enough to insist on the rights afforded them through Islam—rights like financial independence and support, and protection from sexist and unequal divisions of labor in the home. Skewed societal beliefs and restraints prevent a woman from having two very important and indispensable tools for a satisfying life—a modicum of financial independence, and a reasonable level of free time with which to pursue any semblance of a true and authentic calling.

Often women, especially Muslim women, are reduced to "reading while waiting for the iron to heat," as poet Adrienne Rich writes in her *Portrait of a Daughter-in-law*. We are continually trying to squeeze the pulls of the heart between the more "legitimate" and practical cares and responsibilities of day to day life. The sad thing about this tendency is the mistaken assumption that, through the neglect of ourselves, we can better serve the ones we love.

To make matters worse, too many Muslim men consider the pinnacle of womanhood to be buried in impossible ideals, in which, like the Roman poet Horace, women are considered highly only so long as they remain, "*Dulce ridens, dulce loquens*"—Sweetly laughing, sweetly speaking. She may be anything; a doctor, lawyer, businesswoman, scientist, *that's fine,* but only if she may also, *and first*, be beautiful, pleasing, self-effacing, and proficient in catering to *all of the wants* of her husband and family, *whether they be her Islamic responsibility* or not.

There is no question that doors have been opened for women where they once stood bolted. We, for the most part, are free to pursue our dreams. The only problem is that we have not been freed, nor have we freed ourselves, from one iota of the baseless responsibility heaped upon the generations before us—generations for whom the door remained bolted. The result is that we are placed in the cruel position of being able to glimpse our dreams, our natural abilities, talents and potential, yet are so strained for time and resources that at best we can only produce a half-hearted attempt at their fulfillment.

Florence Nightingale spoke to the heart of this issue in her writings, and had a keen insight on the lives of married women, women whose responsibilities and family pulls are of such an overwhelming nature as to prove insurmountable. She wrote,

> When shall we see a woman make a study of what she does? Married women cannot; for a man would think, if his wife undertook any great work with the intention of carrying it out—of making anything but a sham out of it—that she should suckle his fools [Othello] and "chronicle his small beer" less well for it—that he would have not so good a dinner—that she would destroy, as it is called, his domestic life.

You may say, dear reader, as I did, "But...my husband is not like that...I am not like that. I can both 'undertake great work' and carry it out." Perhaps that is true. But I ask you, then, *can* you do it without guilt and without interruption? (Admit it, you find "without interruption" smacking of selfishness. I know I do—I have babies pulling at my skirts, a husband with a rumbling stomach, a Pepsi stain in the rug just waiting to be scrubbed out, and friends to call). Is there really a block of time in your day in which you can engage in your "soul's task?" Can you, with clear conscience, argue with Florence Nightingale's observation that,

> Women are never supposed to have any occupation of sufficient importance not to be interrupted, except 'suckling their fools'; and women themselves have accepted this, have written books to support it, and have trained themselves so as to consider whatever they do as not of such value to the world or to others, but they can throw it up at the first claim of 'social life'.

I submit that this is exactly the lot of the vast majority of Muslim women, that their abilities above and beyond the domestic realm are largely sacrificed, and that the Quranic verse, "Men are the protectors and maintainers of women...because they provide for them out of their sustenance," has been interpreted as a *limitation* on their pursuits rather than an emancipation. For, Islamic pundits the world over, expound on the delicate, imperiled, and weak nature of women, and view the "protection" verse as justification for virtual enslavement. They reason that women logically ransom their "room and board" with domestic and family responsibility to the exclusion of all else.

Not only is this injustice in the extreme (after all, the relative monetary and provisioning value assigned to the endurance of such wifely duties as childbirth and years of sleepless nights never enters into the equation), but it carries with it the real result of placing literally more than half of the Muslim population veritably out of commission when it comes to sharing what they have to offer to the community and the world.

Pericles, the Athenian statesman, wrote in the fifth century, "The chief glory of woman is not to be talked of." Can we really, in clear conscience, argue that this is not widely the greatest common ideal in Islamic womanhood today? If you doubt this, dear reader, consider for a moment whether a woman rising up, offering her voice, talent, wisdom and knowledge in the mosque or community fares well. Although, she may, for a while, be listened to, perhaps even tolerated, after any length of time, rumblings will start—She is loud, she is "bossy," she should be home making dinner. The schism between the propaganda of the emancipated Islamic woman and the culturally bound reality rears its head. In the words of Virginia Woolf,

> ...A very queer, composite being emerges. Imaniginatively, she is of the highest importance; she pervades poetry from cover to cover; she is all but absent from history. She dominates the lives of kings and conquers in fiction; in fact she was the slave of any boy whose parents forced a ring on her finger....A worm winged like an eagle; the spirit of life and beauty in the kitchen chopping up suet.

If we honestly face the mirror, is our collective reality as Muslim women really so different from what Virginia Woolf describes? Can we, within our own circles and freed from the pressure to provide a good image to the "outside world" admit that the *reality* of the perception of what makes a "good woman" is so far removed from the Islamic ideal that something must be done about it?

In our zeal to protect our religion, and to always present it in the light it deserves, we are often the first to repeat, ad naseum, "That is not Islam...It is Arab, Persian, Pakistani culture...There is a difference!"

Okay...so, fine and good. But what about our *realities*, our day-to-day lives that must crash again and again against the walls of culture as surely and relentlessly as the waves of the sea pounding the shore?

In a mode where we have abandoned our authenticity, we are ripe candidates, completely vulnerable to the tyranny of cultural prejudice and injustice. Yet, how can a woman, such as Florence Nightingale describes, find the strength to uphold the banner of authenticity, to claim all that is rightfully hers to experience in life, and hers to uniquely provide for others? How can she resist the relentless draw of conformity in order to become the full embodiment of the Islamic Woman as she was meant to be, without feeling inside that it is a sham and a show? Must we be like the women Nightingale describes,

> Women dream till they have no longer the strength to dream; those dreams against which they so struggle, so honestly, vigorously, and contentiously, and so in vain, yet, which are their life, without which they could not have lived; those dreams go at last. All their plans and visions seem vanished, and they know not where; gone, and they cannot recall them. They do not even remember them. And they are left without the reality of (food) or of hope.
>
> Later in life, they neither desire nor dream, neither of activity, nor of love, nor of intellect. The last one often survives the longest. They wish if their experience could benefit anybody, to give them to someone. But they never find an hour free in which to collect their thoughts, and so discouragement becomes ever deeper and deeper, and they less and less capable of undertaking anything.

A woman does not become the kind of woman "without the strength to dream" from completely external forces. The real influence, the force that exerts the greatest pressure arises from within—for, we, as women, especially as Muslim women, accept, *even embrace* all kinds of lies that so obviously fly in the face of self-interest, both individually, and collectively, that it is obvious we are bartering something in exchange.

Simone Weil said, "All sins are attempts to fill voids."

I would go farther and say, not only sins, but a certain vulnerability to untruth as well.

Too often, we willingly barter self-respect, health, freedom, and ultimately integrity, in a desperate attempt to "fill the void" of our souls. Women readily accept untruths about the definition of what it means to be a "good woman"—put themselves down, damper their intelligence, cultivate airs of weakness, and engage in meaningless frivolity, in attempts to flatter and appear non-threatening—and for this, gain acceptance.

Many women work themselves to the point of exhaustion, engaging in the mad search for approval that is ultimately paid for with the sacrifice of joy, irretrievable time and health, and steadfastly live for the occasionally dropped complement like a cat hoping for scraps at a dining room table. Still others use their personal freedom as collateral against a loan of esteem and the good opinion of others, not realizing that personal honor best resides within the harbor of individual integrity—in whose calm waters it is an asset that cannot, as when placed in the hands of others, be revoked quickly and without recourse on the slightest breath of gossip, however unfounded.

My personal choice in my search for approval included a subscription to the modern torture manual, *Martha Stewart's Living*.

Come hell or high water, I would have the "perfect home"; the cleanest, most ordered, the best, most time consuming meals, the most pristine garden and happiest family. I would be heralded near and far as the model of Islamic wifedom. When complements occasionally rolled my way, I would bask in them like a model for Bain de Soleil.

My homemaking efforts were tireless and legendary—rolling grape leaves by the hundred (a dish, in my opinion, that rivals the most complicated and complete Thanksgiving dinner in the frustrating schism between the effort required in its preparation and the speed of its consumption), repair a piece of furniture, care for my children, drive my son to speech therapy (forty-five minutes each way), return home, clean the house (comet clean, mind you), put the grape leaves on to cook, give my daughter a bath, fold the laundry, scrub the kitchen floor, then hurry to the bathroom to apply a fresh layer of lipstick as my husband's key turned in the door (Oh, and did I mention the fresh pear tart baking in the oven for dessert?).

To the average Muslim man, this sounds great…just about everything you could wish for in a wife…except…Except I was so tired and cranky by six o'clock no one would be surprised to see my head spin around, *a la exorcist*. Oh, yeah, I looked nice, all apron-clad and "How was your day, dear?"—But, look at me sideways and my sweet, angelic, *What can I do for you?* voice could just as easily turn into a disembodied satanic shriek faster than you can say, "What's for dinner?"

I was horrible, and, although my home is covered in thick, pristine cream carpeting (with two young children and a husband in the home, just another testimony to my madness), it could just as well have been eggshells for all of the careful treading required to be around me, head intact.

Not only did I impose unrealistic demands on myself (my husband would have been just as happy with a bowl of *Top Ramen* and a drawer full of clean underwear), but I also placed those demands on other women around me, both in focusing a critical eye on those who didn't measure up to my stringent demands of perfection, and in my portrayal of a dishonest image of effortless hearthside bliss while, underneath disharmony and tension reigned.

In contrast, my sister-in-law was the polar opposite.

Refusing to sell her own happiness wholesale for the approval of others, she possessed the uncanny and rare ability to draw the line between genuine, reasonable responsibility and the optional. For example, not afraid to leave a pile of dishes in the sink after dinner, she has the audacious ability to say, "I want to rest, too. They can wait." She doesn't obsess about the dust on the shelves, or even the dirty laundry piling up. In fact, she rarely has dinner waiting on the table when her husband returns from work. Horror of horrors, her husband even makes his own tea.

Boy, did she bug me.

For the first few years I knew her, the derision I felt toward this woman and her "laziness" was only diminished by the satisfaction I gained from the occasional complement sent my way at her expense—"We're so glad you're not like her!"

Then one day, while listening to the television while doing the dishes (I never had the time to actually watch the television of course), I heard the statement, "What bothers you in others is usually exactly the same thing you need to work on in yourself."

This statement brought to mind a similar idea expressed by a Muslim friend about the *hadith*, "The believer is the believer's mirror...(Abu-Dawud, 41: 4900)."

At the time, a friend told me she believed this to mean exactly the same thing as I had just heard on the television, and, although, then, I had no clue about what she was getting at, for the first time, I now began to recognize the point of what she was saying. For some reason, as I stood there, hands busily scrubbing away, I thought of my sister-in-law, and my attitude toward her; an attitude that I was beginning to realize was strangely hostile and even competitive.

I wondered why I felt so much satisfaction when someone criticized her, and why her lifestyle bothered me so much when it didn't affect my life in any way.

For the first time, as I reached under the sink to retrieve a much coveted pack of fresh Brillo pads (was that a puddle of water under there?), the thought, *rather stealthily*, crept into my mind that it might not be an accident that what I found to be difficult, annoying, or frustrating in others (like my sister-in-law), or, on the other hand, what I admired to the point of jealousy, may be appearing as reflections of things I have to learn in my own life.

Ah, Zen and the job of doing dishes—a meditative technique of women throughout the ages. Snow-white fingernails aren't the only fringe benefit of foregoing the dishwasher (Ok, so it was on the fritz...I digress...).

My sister-in-law possessed a refreshingly open and honest personality of the kind that is as rare to encounter (especially in Muslim circles) as an alien spaceship, while I, for all my blustering about wanting to know and befriend people who were honest and genuine, was annoyed by her to no end.

I slowly realized that I wasn't annoyed with her and her habits, as much as I was threatened—threatened by her life of authenticity, ability to cling to a sense of the genuine, her conscious refusal to exhaust herself to please others, and her continued tendency to retain a semblance of a life for herself in spite of tremendous pressure (pressure of which I am ashamed to admit, I was a source). She threatened me and my choice to live otherwise. After all, there was no question that for all my efforts I certainly looked the part of the pristine, dutiful, bashful, and hard-working Muslim woman (at least according to cultural expectations of what that entails). The reality, however, was that few had a better grip on the genuine essence of what it means to be an authentic Muslim woman than my sister-in-law—who not only knew all of her rights, *but actually took them* come what may, without apology or sugar coating.

The fact that women like my sister-in-law are, in all honesty, quite rare is not surprising. The truth is, membership in club self-sacrifice is at an all time high given all of the Muslim women swelling its ranks. We could have a convention, give seminars in "womanly duties," make baklava, and roll grape leaves till the break of dawn. This is simply because the climate of cultural expectation in which we live provides an incomparably rich environment for inauthenticity and the soul-killing self-sacrifice that makes the pursuit of genuine passions, interests and talent—our real woman's work, all but impossible.

Sadly, the greatest tragedy of all of this, is that hollow portrayals of ideal womanhood are lauded while real honesty is the focus of derision. The result is that the far reaches of the more than half of the population of the Islamic world is all but untapped, to the detriment of women and men. As Tennyson wrote in *The Princess,* "If she be small, slight natured, miserable, how shall men grow?"

Far from advocating the need for a public relations campaign, or an international call to arms for the women of the Islamic world to throw off the chains of sexist expectation and embark on the pressing work of their souls, I believe the only way for change to begin is in the individual heart. Without first developing the strength to resist the pull of the "acceptance and approval trade" in favor of what we internally know to be good and true, it is pointless to attempt to change the expectations of others, and of society as a whole. It is in the power of the individual heart not only to refuse to judge ourselves by false standards of "goodness" but also to refuse to judge other women as well—this is the basis for meaningful change, change that does more than scratch the surface.

Yet, how do we develop this strength?

First, we must acknowledge that it is not enough to attempt a change through will alone. We all know "will-power" never has enough power behind it to last for more than a week. Instead, we must focus on filling the "voids of the soul," the voids that prompt us to barter our authenticity in the first place. Only a whole woman, and only a strong woman can be a friend to her sisters, and her real work in life—her true passions, and her true self. All she has to offer to others through utilization of the unique gifts that are hers remain dormant until she finally begins to fill the voids of her soul. Only then can she be strong, and only then can she be freed from the yawning dissatisfaction of an unauthentic life, however good it appears on the surface.

There are three concrete steps that can help to create a personal environment that is conducive to the pursuance of a fulfilling and satisfying life—the kind of life that not only benefits the woman, her family, and ultimately her society, but also creates the kind of integrity in which faith can truly flourish.

First, it is extremely important to acknowledge the aspects of self that have been leached out of existence in trade for acceptance. I am not referring to the ways in which we strive to please others out of a sense of genuine satisfaction, joy, and responsibility, but, instead, to all of those ways in which we satisfy others and feel a quiet, internal voice of resentment. I like to consider that voice, the rumbling, discontented feeling that we are being taken advantage of, as an internal alarm, a signal that alerts us to the fact that we are selling something—work, time, energy, opinion, personality, or true belief, in exchange for the esteem of others. The voice is an asset, and once you begin tuning into that signal, you will find it gets louder, more clear, and easier to recognize as time goes by—easier to recognize and thankfully harder to ignore.

A useful exercise is to make a list of all of the times you can think of when you hear, or have heard, this alarm—a list for your eyes only, and a list that requires a strenuous, but freeing search of the heart for all of the things you currently do and become without genuine joy, belief, and generosity of spirit. You will find it surprising, when you finish, to see all of the countless ways you barter your resources—time, energy, money, integrity, and talent, out of something other than a genuine, internal desire to do so.

It helps to go for a solitary walk, to think about the reasons for your individual barter system. What do you seek in exchange? Approval, esteem, love, acceptance? Is it working? Or is it draining your resources—physical, emotional, and spiritual?

Second in importance, another step that is seldom discussed, not popular to acknowledge, and often painful to accept for Muslim women in particular, is the role some measure of financial independence plays in the feeling of identity and autonomy within the world.

Islam has a strong position on the financial independence and rights of women—women are not only free to earn, acquire, and retain their own money, but are allowed protection from appropriation from the men in their lives. Unfortunately, as in most things, the reality is quite different.

Too often women are shamed, cajoled, coerced, and otherwise convinced to give over any and all financial stores for a variety of supposed reasons. Often, this is just another manifestation of the "disease to please," to be well thought of, to appear unselfish, helpful, generous, and willing to contribute to the "good of the family," or whatever other supposed "good" is at hand.

Few women, or men for that matter, realize the very negative repercussions that come from the loss of self-esteem and identity that directly result from the want of some kind of financial independence, be it even a token amount. The positive effect of even a small change in this area cannot be underestimated.

Consider the words of Alexandra Stoddard, in her book *Mothers: A Celebration:*

> ...In order to maintain the integrity of our independence and keep the flame of our own identity lit, it is helpful to have our own money. This is an observation that may make many at-home mothers uneasy. Although some mothers who do not work outside the home may have happily made their decision to stay home with their children, many probably still experience some anxiety about not having money that is entirely theirs to use at their own discretion. Many women have told me that, although they have never regretted their choice not to work outside the home, it is very difficult not having their own money. What's the remedy for this very prevalent situation?
>
> The most obvious answer is to earn your own money. This may be "easier said than done", but today there are more options for

earning money at home....The goal isn't to find your life's calling in a job, but to give you a greater sense of freedom by making your own money....Earning your own money can be extremely restorative, even if it's a small amount each week.

My own experience has shown me the wisdom of Stoddard's words.

Early in my marriage, I had no financial independence. This is not to say that I had no money. In fact, my husband was quite generous and allowed me full access to our joint bank account. However, although I did not feel deprived financially, I did miss the feeling of having my own money, for which I alone was responsible.

Later, in an attempt to save money, I suggested we budget our grocery money into a separate account (mine), and any money left over (from meticulous meal planning and coupon use) was mine to save or use at my discretion.

Not only did this arrangement save money and reduce waste, but it gave me a renewed sense of independence and accomplishment. The fact was, I actually had less money to spend than when I operated from a joint account, but I was satisfied with less because it had the added dignity of being *mine*.

Having my own discretionary funds has given me new incentive to find more ways to be financially independent.

It has been written that, "to have some stay in this uncertain world that cannot be undermined is of the utmost consequence." I couldn't agree more.

If you don't have independent funds, I urge you to come up with some ideas on how you might procure "some stay"—be it twenty dollars a month, as long as it "cannot be undermined"—(the internet and bookstore are excellent resources for ideas). Try this and I am sure you will find the psychological rewards to be surprising.

If financial independence is beneficial to the encouragement of an internal sense of autonomy, an autonomy necessary to pursue individual and passionate "souls work," the actual funds can prove helpful.

For me, pens, paper, cappuccino, printer ink, and trips to the bookstore, the physical components of my love of writing, come from my own funds. The satisfaction of this is enormous. If you think this petty, either you have never been without independent funds, or you currently *are* and have never lived otherwise. I urge you to try it and see what a difference it makes.

The third and most important step toward becoming a woman capable of realizing and following a "souls work" is also the most difficult. It involves freeing up sufficient time with which to pursue a personal calling without, as Florence Nightingale said, "making a sham out of it."

This step involves a ruthlessness seldom seen amongst the "gentler sex"—a ruthlessness that requires nothing short of murder.

It often seems, as we go through out days that time is devoured by all the demands placed upon us. The rigors of marriage, motherhood, and the vast array of responsibilities that must be reckoned with without choice or option—the thousand sacrifices we make for the benefit of others—devour the minutes of the day until we feel we have nothing left for anything more ambitious than a five minute bath (with a toddler banging on the door).

The only remedy to this involves utter ruthlessness.

When Virginia Woolf, the great twentieth century writer, began her career, she found that she came against a powerful adversary—so powerful that it had to be slain for her to continue. She called this adversary "the angel in the house."

She wrote;

> It was she who bothered me and wasted my time and so tormented me that at last I killed her… –You may not know what I mean by the angel in the house. I will describe her as short as I can. She was intensely sympathetic. She was intensely charming. She was utterly unselfish. She excelled in the difficult arts of family life. She sacrificed herself daily. If there was chicken she took the leg; if there were a draught she sat in it—in short, she was so constituted that she never had a mind or a wish of her own but preferred to sympathize always with the minds and wishes of others…

It is this angel that kills everything authentic within, and it is this angel that sneaks in when we are writing, reading, sewing, learning, playing, *living*, to say, "Not now…later. There is work to be done, someone to please."

Perhaps it would be a small thing; perhaps there would be room for the angel in the house would she stay small, reasonable, kind in her demands. But the sad fact is that, once allowed in through the door of insecurity, she grows to such a size as to allow nothing else, especially anything resembling self-care, to survive. She kills with her kindness and, like a parasite, takes all, leaving nothing but a bitter, bewildered shell of all that we were—all fire, ambition and hope gone.

The important thing to realize about her, this angel, is that she is not evoked by those she serves so religiously, those loved ones we imagine reap the benefits of her service. She is evoked from within; evoked when we worry that we are not "good enough," when we allow petty trivialities to reign in our hearts. In such an atmosphere, she will storm in and kill.

It is necessary, therefore, to do as Virginia Woolf finally did and slay her first.

How do we do that?

Unfortunately, Woolf didn't detail her method. However, I have a strong suspicion half of the battle is in the mere recognition of the existence of your angel. Calling her by her name heralds the beginning of her demise.

The final blow is more complicated, however, and, like death by arsenic, requires a series of small, steady doses—doses of self-confidence, assertion and care. It is the consistency, the continual effort that kills her in the end.

This final step involves another crime, for not only must we murder our angel—lest she kill us, but we must steal as well.

It takes time to embark on a "souls work." For that matter, it takes time for many of us to rediscover just what our souls work is. Many of us have so buried our original dreams and personalities under so many layers of responsibilities, false expectations and disguises, that we genuinely feel we don't have a clue about our heart's passion. Is it any wonder we can scarcely bring ourselves to pray? We have so lost sight of who we are that we are coming to prayer without our hearts.

The only way to find passion for living—authentic passion for the life we were meant to live, is by stealing time to go after it.

You may protest, thinking, "there is no time…I have babies, a job, a family, a sick parent, fields to plow…"

Let me assure you there *is* time. You must cheat and steal it away. The reality is, you are only stealing it from your angel anyway. We must recognize the shattering truth that, unlike most men, the majority of women's lives are spent, not in the acquisition of grand schemes, goals and efforts, but in the thousand small details of the day. Some of these details can be forsaken, and time can be stolen away from them. Leave the dishes, simplify housekeeping, get rid of clutter, don't keep the "perfect" lawn, stop saying "yes" *all the time* to *everything*. Think of it as stealing, feel naughty—keep it a secret and work on yourself for a change. Believe it or not, everyone you love will benefit, including you. Your souls work will become apparent and grow—and your relationship with God and faith will blossom.

Zealously take time—read, write, walk, think and explore. Live a truly authentic life as a Muslim woman—the life you were meant to live, and a life in which you have something of real value to offer. To live anything else is a waste and a lie. Robert Louis Stevenson wrote, "To be what we are, and to become what we are capable of becoming, is the only end in life." Once we really strive to become that, once we give up all the pretense we have built up around ourselves, we are finally capable of bringing ourselves to a true and honest faith—for we are finally present—as Martin Luther said, "Here I stand. I can do no other. God help me. Amen."

Epilogue

"Please tell me... Is it a painful death?"

--"No. He will simply slip into a sleep
...he will essentially die in his sleep."

(Conversation with my son's doctor –Children's Hospital, February, 2001)

I finished writing this book at the end of January.

February began with furious editing, devouring my time and my sanity (such as it is). Thus, it was with a bit more than the standard frustration when I realized my children were coming down with yet another cold that would require my immediate attention.

My daughter bounced back with her usual ease, after a week of sniffles, while my son exhibited his equally usual tenacity in hanging onto his particular bug with an iron grip (usually only loosened with a solid round of antibiotics). This in mind, I didn't worry when his illness persisted, seemed to move onto stomach flu for a few days, then abated to a generalized fatigue.

I remember him sleeping next to me in my bed, as I banished errors from my manuscript on my husband's laptop. It had been literally years since he had taken a nap, and I was surprised, but grateful to have the time to work—although, I do remember thinking it strange.

It was only when it snowed for the first time of the year—and my, usually boundlessly energetic, boy refused to go outside to play, that I began to suspect that perhaps everything was not normal. Then I began to notice the yellow tinge to his eyes.

When he awoke the next day, covered in a rash, I loaded him off to his pediatrician, who performed blood tests diagnosing him with Hepatitis A. She assured me that it was about as serious as "food poisoning," and would eventually resolve itself.

A day later, the doctor called me with the news that they had been in error. My son did not have Hepatitis A, but instead "general hepatitis."

I was terrified.

"What does that mean?" I asked, immediately assuming he had the more serious Hepatitis B, or C. "Isn't that more serious?"

"No." she assured me. "It simply means his liver is inflamed by a simple virus." "He is probably already in the recovery stage."

The next day, as I sat in the bathroom, watching him splash in his bath, I noticed he had become so yellow all over that if I held my highlighter pen next to his skin *they matched*. I immediately decided to take him to the emergency room for another opinion.

When the emergency room doctor walked into the room with the results of more blood tests in her hand, I immediately saw concern on her face. She said, "You need to take your son to Children's Hospital RIGHT NOW." "Ibrahim is very ill, and neither I, nor your doctor know what is going on here with his liver."

Thus began a whirlwind of disbelief, beginning with the attending physician at Children's reply to my question, "How concerned should I be right now?"

"Well, Mrs. Jones…Ill be honest with you." He said. "Your son is showing signs of significant acute liver disease. Right now we don't know what it is, and we are going to admit him tonight. Either he will recover, or he will progress to liver failure, need a transplant, or he will die."

Three days later, in a dimly lit parent conference room, I sat across from a liver specialist telling me that, indeed, my son's liver was failing, and it was time to evaluate him for a liver transplant.

Once again, the pain without relief was in my life, and the words from my chapter, "When Things are Bad" seemed to float in front of my eyes. Yet, that first week, I couldn't bring myself to even acknowledge words of any kind. I could only sleep beside my son—my baby who could no longer summon the strength to hold a crayon, was suffering through days of vomiting, painful procedures, blood transfusions, and blood-ammonia levels so high that his breath burned my nose with its chemical smell, and blindly stare at the pattern on the hospital carpeting.

After that first week, however, when the shock began to abate, I began to wonder at the words I had written about suffering. I waited to see what would happen, almost as a spectator. I wondered, Would God get us through this? Was it really true that God never gives us more than we can bear?

Like most mothers, my children are my absolute loves, and, by extension, so are all children.

Epilogue

Before, the thought of children suffering in any way—or the image of their suffering, on the news, in books, or even photographs, was more than I could handle. If I happened to see a child, even by accident, suffering on television, I would be depressed to the point of despair *for days*. The thought of being in a children's hospital, filled with suffering, sick and dying children was something I could not imagine.

Now, not only was I in a children's hospital for days on end, seeing babies, toddlers, and older children bald from chemotherapy, paralyzed from accidents, crippled with birth defects, and recovering from surgeries, but I was standing, giving comfort to my child, looking up at me with his terrified eyes as they took yet another draw of blood from his little body.

It was my baby who was dying. My son who I loved without end. How could God make this Ok?

Slowly, quietly watching and surviving moment to moment, I began to realize that, somehow, God just was. He was making it Ok. Not in any way that can be described, but in a silent, miraculous way—a way that defied explanation or words of any kind. It simply was not more than I, or we could bear—although it should have been.

Again, as a spectator, I often would look down at my hands and wonder, am I going to lose it now? Am I going to run, screaming into oblivion, trying to jump out of my skin, my reality? Always, the answer was no.

My son was screaming—I was there for him, soothing him, and it was working.

The doctor was telling us that he was deteriorating—My husband and I took turns crying, and we could come back into the room with unexplainable hope.

We were surviving the unsurvivable, and God really was comforting us—really was comforting my son.

We were in the hospital for one month and one week. Ibrahim was listed for a transplant after the sixth day. If a liver came, he would get it. His doctor, the head of Gastroenterology, and the transplant surgeon explained that they could find no cause for his liver failure, but believed it was a unidentifiable virus killing his liver cells. They said they saw about four cases of liver failure a year with about fifty percent of unknown cause. Of those cases none, in their experience, had ever recovered. They were either transplanted, or died.

We gave the go-ahead for a transplant if a liver became available.

One didn't. One week later, Ibrahim began a recovery the likes of which they had never seen in a child with liver failure at Children's Hospital—a miracle both in itself, and in the fact that a donor didn't come before the recovery.

Today it is two months since the first day of his hospitalization, and he is playing in the back yard with his sister. He is no longer yellow, and, aside from the small scars from his IV lines, you would never believe he was in the ICU fighting for his life just five weeks ago.

It's hard to explain how I feel about his recovery, or his sudden illness.

It seems strange to say, but I am immensely glad it happened—and not only because of the miraculous outcome, but also because of the sure knowledge that has replaced the fear that reigned in my heart at the time I wrote, "When Things are Bad."

Then, I knew that bad things happen in life, and that God promised not to give a soul greater pain than it is capable of withstanding—but, lets just say I harbored some doubt, especially after my son's brush with Autism and Fragile X.

The fact that God once again used my beloved son to convince me of this truth is, to me, a clear sign that he really wanted me to get the point. I have nothing to fear. God will not give me (or you) more than can be borne. Thank God, I now know that. I am even more astonished that God gave me such a lesson, and allowed me to keep my son with me as well—just another proof, Most Gracious, Most Merciful.

Alhamdullah...Thank you, God.

J. Lynn Jones
April, 2001